Y TOO YOUNG

O TO BE OLD

Secrets from Bible Seniors on How to Live Long and Well

John Gilmore

Harold Shaw Publishers
Wheaton, Illinois

Copyright © 1992 by John Gilmore

ISBN 0-87788-839-6

Library of Congress Cataloging-in-Publication Data

Gilmore, John, 1934–
   Too young to be old : secrets from Bible seniors on how to live
long and well / John Gilmore.
     p.   cm.
   Includes bibliographical references.
   ISBN 0-87788-839-6
   1. Aged in the Bible. 2. Aged—Religious life. 3. Old age—Biblical
teaching. I. Title.
BS680.A34G54 1992   92-11383
220.9′2′0846—dc20   CIP

---

99 98 97 96 95 94 93 92

10 9 8 7 6 5 4 3 2 1

Dedicated
to
Leslie Lynn Webster
John Owen Gilmore
Martyn Edward Gilmore

"I have no greater joy than to hear that my children
are walking in the truth."
3 John 4

"Grow old along with me!
The best is yet to be,
The last of life, for which the first was made:
Our times are in His hand
Who saith 'A whole I planned,
Youth shows but half; trust God: see all nor be afraid!' "
Robert Browning (1812-1889)
"Rabbi Ben Ezra"

Contents

Acknowledgments _____ *vii*

Preface_____ *ix*

1. Secrets of Long Life _____ *1*

2. Biblical Records of Long Life _____ 21

3. Job: A Senior Who Confessed in Print _____ 33

4. Abraham: A Senior Who Trusted _____ 41
God's Abundance

5. Sarah: A Senior Whose Laughter _____ 51
Was Revealing

6. Moses: A Senior Homebody _____ 61

7. Caleb: A Senior Dynamo _____ 73

8. Naomi: A Senior Who Trusted God _____ 87
in Tough Times

9. Barzillai: A Senior Who Served God _____ 99
despite the Dangers

10. David: A Senior Who Applauded God _____ 111

11. Solomon: A Senior Poet Who Gave a _____ 121
Pep Talk

12. Zechariah: A Senior Who Faced _____ 135
Frustration

13. Simeon: A Senior Blessed by Vision_____ 145

14. Anna: A Senior Who Faced Grief_____ 155

A Senior Prayer _____ 167

Notes _____ 169

Acknowledgments

I wish to thank the following persons for information or comments:

David P. Beal, D. Min., Newton Bush, Th.D., Tom Dryer, M.D., Ken Kregel, Donald Leggett, Th.D., James H. Lloyd, Library Director, Cincinnati Bible College and Seminary, June Schlef, Gail Terrell, Ph.D., Patricia A. Wolfe, Activity Director, Three Rivers Convalescent Center, Cincinnati.

Preface

I WAS FIRST DRAWN TO THE SUBJECT OF SENIORS BECAUSE OF my mother, the late Anna Gilmore, of Souderton, Pennsylvania. After my father's death she found healing, friendships, and fellowship in her involvement at the Senior Adult Activity Center of Indian Valley, Pennsylvania.

It was a surprise to find out that she entered a senior beauty contest at the age of 79! After competing and winning in her own area, she went on to competition at the state level. There she was one of eleven finalists. In Atlantic City she won the 1980 state title "Ms. Senior America of Pennsylvania" over ten younger senior women. In addition, she won "Ms. Congeniality." One reporter described her eyes as "Rice Crispy eyes" because they seemed to "snap, crackle, and pop with animation."

For her talent entry she sang "Alice Blue Gown" in (what else but) a blue gown made by my sister, Mary

Anna. My family and I were happy to share in the festive banquet at the Indian Valley Center. Later she was proud to show off pictures from her cruise to the Bahamas, one of the contest prizes.

My mother opened my eyes to burgeoning senior events and causes. She was an unofficial ambassador for seniors where she lived. In competition she shared her personal vibrancy with others.

Increasingly, seniors flock together in independent living centers or retirement communities, now numbering more than 15,000 nationwide. That number doesn't include the nursing homes or convalescent centers (skilled and intermediate care facilities) of which there are some 18,000! In long-term care facilities, 71 percent of residents are over 75 years old.

A widespread misconception is that the majority of the elderly are institutionalized. At the present time in the U.S., only about 5 percent of the elderly reside in institutions of one kind or another.

By far the oldest "senior centers" have been churches. Many seniors still manage their homes alone and they enjoy going to church both on Sunday and during the week. Retirees find second careers as volunteer workers in churches.

Recently my attention has been redirected toward seniors. I'm now on the outer edges of that category. In addition, I've been noticing more seniors in the Bible, possibly because I see more seniors in church.

Madisonville Baptist Church, which I pastor, is probably representative of many churches in America. The percentage of the congregation made up by seniors is growing.

The older we grow the more we feel drawn to seniors in the Scriptures. Over the last six years I've shared my findings about some of the great seniors in Scripture. Response to these mini-biographies has been positive.

When I expressed the hope of someday submitting my studies as a book, everyone was enthusiastic about their usefulness.

Football fields or basketball courts are measured spaces. In addition, each game is only so long. Similarly, print fills pages of prescribed size so that readers are not overtaxed. To prevent overcrowding, some scriptural seniors have been omitted. I apologize if your favorites are not here.

I hope that these studies of Bible seniors will act like Vitamin B-12 shots. I pray that what's ahead will show the attractive individuality of Bible seniors in their struggles, stresses, and successes. I also pray that you will be inspired by them to keep active in life and in growing as a Christian.

Before being transported into the worlds of the Old and New Testaments, permit me to insert a word of thanks to all the seniors, past and present, who have contributed to my life. I hope this book qualitatively contributes to *their* lives. And, I hope everyone catches the realism, individualism, and inspiration of the Bible seniors whose lives are reviewed here.

Dr. John Gilmore
May 16, 1992
The Kērux Kabin*
P.O. Box 24064
Cincinnati, OH 45224

---

*"Kērux" is the transliterated Greek word for "herald"; "Kabin" the Germanized English western word for "house." Organizations, churches, and individuals may contact me at the above address.

1

Secrets of Long Life

We have no more right to shorten our own
than another's life, and the duty of
self-preservation which instinct teaches,
is one which the Bible enforces.
THOMAS GUTHRIE, *Memoirs*

If the Bible does not often speak directly *to* the elderly,
it still has some significant things to say *about* aging,
the aged, and their proper treatment.
STEPHEN SAPP, *Full of Years*

O<small>N NBC'S "TODAY"</small> SHOW WILLARD SCOTT RECOGNIZES elderly Americans on their birthdays. Hurrah! Affirming the aging gives a shot in the arm to any senior viewers who might be thinking about throwing in the towel!

Reaching a ripe old age deserves recognition. But knowing how to live long is a mystery, a challenge, and sometimes a problem. Short lives are enigmatic and the secrets to long life are elusive.

The older we get the more we empathize with the seniors in Scripture. Perhaps they can give us safe guidelines on aging. The Bible is one book where seniors, good and bad, are seen for who they were and how they lived.

The Old Testament, especially, astonishes us with its array of seniors. That so many are recorded in Scripture is proof that God, the Ancient of Days, never showed a whiff of ageism. God seems to have played a trick on the obsessively youth-oriented when he included old people in the glorious event of Christ's birth, as well as other major happenings throughout biblical history.

When Is a Person Old?

What is old? When is a person a senior? We tend to think of seniors as retired persons. But retirement can be early or late. Some are retired by age fifty-five; others work into their eighties. Retirement can't be the way to measure age, but it can qualify one for the title of "senior citizen."

In Old Testament Hebrew society, the age at which one was considered a "qualified old" was apparently sixty (Leviticus 27:1-8). Those over sixty years paid a significantly reduced temple tax, an indication that sixty was a semiofficial retirement age in Israel. Levite priests had an earlier retirement. They were to quit at fifty (Numbers 8:24-26) with the option of being part-time. Today the statistical beginning of old age is 65. The year when one becomes "an ancient," however, will range from the eighties into the mid-to-late nineties.

Is it fair to calculate old age as beginning at sixty-five? Individual abilities vary in the sixties and seventies. To automatically conclude that everyone age sixty-five is old is patently untrue and unfair.

> Age is a quality of mind—
> If you have left your dreams behind,
> If hope is lost,
> If you no longer look ahead,
> If your ambitions' fires are dead—
> Then you are old.
> —*Unknown*

People who enjoy life want to be around to enjoy it more. Long life is a worthy goal. What does the Bible say about the secret to living long? Why did people in the Old Testament live so much longer than people do today? After all, aren't today's health aids better? Isn't our knowledge of nutrition superior?

What Contributes to Long Life?

Attributing extended life to God does not mean we are living inside a mythological bubble. God is a greater reality than humanity, and humanity cannot be explained without him. Yet science provides the nuts-and-bolts particulars, the components of long life. Any explanation of longevity that excludes medical facts is unrealistic.

Gerontology means the study of the aged (from the Greek work, *geron*, "old man"), and geriatrics is the healing of the aged (from *geras*, "old age"). The insights and information from these medical disciplines can ease the mind as well as the body.

Modern medicine gives new hope for living longer and better. Life expectancy has steadily increased during the 1900s. The fastest growing segment of United States population is seniors. In 1850, people over 65 made up 2.5 percent of the total population. Fifty years later (1900) those over 65 crept to 4.1 percent of the total population. By 1956 those over 65 jumped to 8.4 percent.

How do the percentages break down into actual people? In 1977 it was estimated that those over 65 were about twenty-three million, three million more than in 1970. In 1991, 13 percent of the population was 65 years old or older. By the year 2000 the U.S. population over 65 years will be surging toward 24 percent! By the turn of the century some 64 million Americans will be over 65 (an increase of 120 percent since 1979).

Women still hold the record for longevity. In 1980 there were one million plus widowers past 54, whereas there were seven million plus widows! Both sexes have a higher life-expectancy in recent decades. Life expectancy in 1900 was 47 years; by 1985 it had jumped to 75 years.

White males who reached age 75 in 1978 could expect to live another 8.6 years, compared to 11.5 for the white female, and surprisingly, 9.9 for the male and 12.5 for the female of other races.[1]

Heredity, habits, and modern medicine

Heredity, over which medicine has only minimal influence, is an important factor in long life. Deep within our psycho-physical matter is a clock set to run so long before it stops. What we do and how we think can turn back, slow up, or stretch out our biological time clocks.

Harmful and healthy habits affect the value of heredity. Proper diet, exercise, and sleep patterns feed into the web of longevity. It is medical science that tells us which ingredients are needed for the efficient functioning of our bodies. Without absorption of nutritious food, the body will not receive its benefits.

But good nutrition is not enough. One can't get estrogen, for instance, from oatmeal cereal. In senior years hormone balances drop. Androgen and estrogen imbalance causes loss of protein absorption. Under a physician's care these can be monitored and adjusted.

Dr. William B. Kountz of Washington University described a 78-year-old woman who came to him bearded, diabetic, and grouchy. She was so mean that she used her wooden leg as a club against her family doctor. After three months on estrogen she became one of the sweetest persons in the hospital. Her beard went away and so did her bullish disposition. She went home happy and easier to live with.[2]

Living into one's nineties will be more common by the twenty-first century. Levodopamine, the drug that produced astonishing recovery in a case dramatized in the movie *Awakenings,* is used with Parkinson's disease patients, as is another drug, Deprenyl. In addition to being effective with Parkinson patients, Deprenyl shows early signs of waking up the human brain and extending an elder's life. It has also shown dramatic improvement in reducing symptoms of aging in those without Parkinson's disease. Substances called "nerve growth factor" show some ability to eliminate typical signs of aging.

Yet to be released by the FDA, the drug Cognex has been shown to have a beneficial effect on short-term memory, both in Altzheimer's patients and in normal people. While precise side effects and degree of efficacy are still being examined, several drug companies are far along in the development of other similar drugs that will certainly be available before the end of this century.

Dr. Ed Schneider, on ABC's "Ninetysomething," said:

I think, as today many people are taking their multi-vitamin pill in the morning, and people with specific diseases take other pills, we'll be taking pills that will allow us to age more successfully and there may be a pill that will allow us to have the same brain power at age 90—it'd be wonderful!—that we had at age 20.[3]

It helps to laugh
Surgeons and physicians continually remind us that patient attitude is an indispensable component in a full recovery and a full life.

Our disposition can make adjustments easier or harder, or make life shorter or longer. Old age can't be cured, but it can be slowed. And a chief aid in that process is one's positive attitude.

People with a happy outlook, who take life as it comes, and who have learned not to be anxious about getting old, have a huge advantage. They see all of life under the purposes and plans of God. When a person can see humor in stiff knees, poor eyesight, hearing loss, and short sleeps, these conditions will be more bearable and less bothersome. Levity is closely linked to longevity.

> " . . . the wonder drug I recommend to all my friends is laughter. It provides the invisible armor we all need to protect us from the stresses of life. I've made a career out of laughing and it's kept me happy and healthy for 88 years."
> —Bob Hope

Susan H. McFadden, in her perceptive article, "Authentic Humor as an Expression of Spiritual Maturity in the Later Years," noted that humor neither denies nor trivializes suffering, but "bursts through suffering" by providing a spiritual interpretation of it. It is trust in the Lord that makes laughter possible.[4]

Senior attitudinal elasticity is captured in humor. Diane Sawyer of ABC News asked 98-year-old Beatrice Wood how she managed to live so long. Beatrice replied: "When people ask me how I happened to live such a long time—because I'm really very old, old, old—my reply is, 'Chocolate and young men' and that solves it."[5]

Beatrice's comment raises the question of whether deprivation or self-indulgence lengthens or shortens life. There's certainly evidence that a poor diet and lack of exercise contribute to shortening life. We've all known the tobacco-chewing, cork-pulling, pipe-puffing oldsters who fairly brag about the excesses of their lives, and how their habits brought them into old age. These folks need a bushel full of modesty and a strong dose of gratitude to God. It is the elder who extols the eternal God who truly models how to live and die.

God the sustainer

God is the key factor in sustaining a person to old age. Even genetic combinations and hereditary patterns are the Lord's doing, who invented natural law and works through it. The Lord who gives life also maintains it.

Christian seniors honor God by witnessing to his goodness, mercy, and daily kindness. The believer recognizes God in the genetic ticking of biological "time clocks." Dependence on the Lord leads to a life of moderation and therefore contentment. One woman wrote:

> I am a young lady of 96 years. And I'm in a home for elderly ladies with board paid as long as I live, but no income. A niece sends me some when she can spare it.
>
> I am sitting on top of the world watching the years go by. Bodily and mentally I am in fine condition, carrying out . . . ideas I have read for the last twenty years since my husband passed on. He is waiting for me to come to him. Doctors say I am bodily and mentally only 60 years. I feel it; I get up in the morning with a prayer for beautiful life. I thank God for this wonderful world. I feel as if I could do the family wash.
>
> God has been good to me through the years, a fine teenager with good parents, and wonderful husband and now a happy widowhood. I am happy. I love life, but am ready to go when God calls me.

Living Right

What does the Bible say about enriching and extending life? We must take the Bible seriously on matters of aging. It's not just a book of old stories about old people. Within its pages we can find God's accounting for long life. And our best response would be to integrate its viewpoint in our discussions on aging.

In Scripture a long life implies a healthy life. "With long life will I satisfy him and show him my salvation" (Psalm 91:16). Especially satisfied are those whose lives know the joy of fellowship with God. "I will call on [God] as long as I live" vowed the psalmist (116:2).

Does living right insure living long? The patriarch Job despaired that evil individuals lived long. Apparently, he felt he would not live long or that the righteous tended to die earlier. He struggled with a sense of divine abandonment: "Why do the wicked live on, growing old and increasing in power?" (Job 21:7).

Psalm 73, similarly, reflected an over-ascription of good health, prosperity, and happiness to the wicked. The psalmist questioned the value of living for God, because the wicked weren't going through hard times as he was (73:4, 13-17).

Another psalm expressed a fear of being discarded (71:9). In Proverbs, the wisdom writer prays that his children will not despise their mother "when she is old" (Proverbs 23:22). Some anxiety is expected when obvious signs of aging appear. Some kinds of depression are brought on by arteriosclerosis, dementia, and other forms of senility. Body chemistry plays a part in why some elderly have a bleak outlook.

Job and the psalmist, it seems, were too generous to the wicked old. They thought of the wicked as hale and hearty when, often, nonbelievers are nastier and more negative than believers of the same age.

W. Somerset Maugham (1874-1965) wrote optimistically about old age when he was sixty:

In old age the taste improves and it is possible to enjoy art and literature without the personal bias that in youth warps the judgment. . . . It is liberated from the trammels of human egoism; free at last, the soul delights in the passing moment, but does not bid it stay.[6]

But in his seventies, when admiring friends wanted to show him respect by sending fruit or flowers for his birthday, he told his secretary to tell them, "It's too late for fruit and too early for flowers!"[7]

Garson Kanin contended Maugham entered his nineties "a broken, bitter, miserable old man—bereft and abandoned by all his relatives, defiant and remorseful by turns."

The Christian, in contrast, has reason to be less crotchety and crabby. Bible-reading elders are continually retaught to view life through the lens of God's perspective. Life's unexpected turns never cease to reaffirm the coordinating influence of God's providence (Romans 8:28). Tedium and agonizing twists can be thankfully received as part of God's plan. In light of God's control of life even modest successes can reverberate with the music of God's goodness.

One component of the equation for living long was built into the Ten Commandments. The command to honor parents had the promise of longevity for children who complied with God's will.

> Honor your father and your mother, so that you may live long in the land the LORD your God is giving you. *Exodus 20:12*

A key feature in this commandment is that God rewards us with our own benefits as we take on the care of our parents. It is a kind of ethical *quid pro quo* (Latin: "this for that"). Being Christians means that we are dedicated to reflective, considerate lifestyles. In turn, this kind of living, generally speaking, will extend life's length. When we honor the source of our lives, we cherish and care for the life he gives us to enjoy.

Jesus warned about the pointlessness of stewing about how long we might or might not live: "Who of you by worrying can add a single hour to his life?" (Matthew 6:27).

Mellow, not "Jello"

One theory about aging is that it mellows us. The radical at age twenty-five may become more conservative at age thirty-five. But at age seventy-one does that person turn into a pussycat or a crank? Or does a nasty alley-cat disposition flair up in an otherwise sleepy house cat? In terms of ideologies, does one go soft or become hardened? Does an old legalist ever mellow? For a sourpuss to mellow would require atrophied smile muscles to loosen up after long years of disuse.

A little more tired at the close of day.
A little less anxious to have our own way;
A little less ready to scold and blame,
A little more care for a brother's good name;
A little less zeal for narrow views,
A little more love for friends proven true.
—*Unknown, altered by author*

Opinions seesaw on this subject. Does age accentuate a person's worst features or smooth the sharp edges? Does a senior become more rigid or more flexible in attitudes? Is there more mellowing or *souring* during the aging process?

Whereas a wife contends her husband at sixty is not the man she knew at twenty and a husband says his bride of twenty was less critical than she is at fifty, the debate rages on from one household to another. We cannot resolve the issue here, but we should look at it.

Professional psychiatrists argue that neuroses and some psychoses burn themselves out with age, and that the rate of mental disorders declines after age seventy.

The person who mellows with age is not declining but developing. Pioneering psychiatrist Carl Jung, who was vigorous until the age of eighty-five, said, "Anyone who fails to go along with life remains suspended, stiff and rigid in mid-air. That is why so many people get wooden in old age; they look back and cling to the past with a secret fear of death in their hearts."[8]

Though muscles and tendons tighten in old age, aging also loosens one's reins on the world. Seniors past seventy seem willing to concede that conclusions need not be held so tightly. Harvard philosopher George Santayana saw himself mellow in later life:

> My old age judges more charitably and thinks better of mankind than my youth ever did. I discount idealization, I forgive one-sidedness, I see that it is essential to perfection of any kind. And in each person I catch the fleeting suggestion of something beautiful, and swear eternal friendship with that.[9]

Mellowing is not a sign of senility. Rather, it's a sign of mental agility combined with tolerance. We become more open to additional options. This doesn't mean that all points of view and systems of belief have become equally valid. (To say that all beliefs are true would be a mellowness turned rotten.)

When our anxiety level is low, we show signs of having mellowed. But we trust God to overrule evil in-

fluences and we look more kindly upon those who strug
gle to absorb and apply Scripture.

The believing seniors of Scripture showed their godly
orientation, not always by the tasks they took on, nor by
how well they did those tasks, *but in their attitude to losses
and in their reaction to change.* In addition, as they
reflected upon past events, they witnessed to God's hand
in them. They encourage us to trust in the Lord, not only
because he is the only redeemer of sinners, but because
he is the great resolver of difficulties. The ancients of the
Old Testament who had the faith of Abraham could not
be ruffled by bad news, for they knew the God who
brought victory out of seeming defeat. James Strachan
notes, ". . . in the ideal old age of the Hebrews one
discerns a grandeur, a meekness, and a mellowness
which was unique."[10]

Mellowness is ripeness *without* rottenness. The unique-
ness of Christian mellowing is the combination of
natural tendencies with spiritual dynamics. The believer
is firm but flexible. The aging senior does not throw out
Christian convictions; he has learned how to embrace
and use them.

The core conviction of God's supremacy allows a
Christian to be less adamant on issues of lesser importance. A mellowed believer has the ability to see God's
action in more situations and in more detail than he or
she saw previously. Such people focus on God's deeds
rather than their own.

Ponder anew
What the Almighty can do
If with his love He befriend Thee.
—*Catherine Winkworth, "Praise to the Lord, the Almighty"*

Confident calm

Psychological stiffness can keep us in a down mood. We may feel worthless and useless. Fear of catastrophic illnesses and of being forgotten can shorten our lives and disable us mentally.

According to physician Dr. Edmund V. Cowley of St. Louis's Washington University, seniors should not fear the process of dying. He reported that in the elderly "pain is so much less acute. Most old people simply drop off to sleep."[11]

But physicians also caution us not to minimize all pain in the elderly. Though they are more often affected by chronic diseases, many of which are not associated with *intense* pain, they find kidney stones, aortic aneurysms, and ruptured gall bladders as painful as does anyone else.

The Christian elderly have other reasons for facing death calmly. David didn't fear death, for he had the Lord with him when he was called to take the lonely path in the narrow channel out of life (Psalm 23:4). The Christian really does not die alone, even when no one is around: He has the Lord leading him home. Even in the "valley of the shadow" God is with us every moment of our departure.

The fear of being useless though alive is even greater than the fear of death. This fear has always been with us:

> Do not cast me away when I am old; do not forsake me when my strength is gone . . . Even when I am old and gray, do not forsake me, O God, till I declare your power to the next generation, your might to all who are to come. *Psalm 71:9, 18*

The Hebrews saw life as a gift from God and long life as a desirable goal. Premature death was unwanted and lamented (Psalm 102:23-24). But God does not guarantee long life to everyone. Our death year is God's secret. It is he who ultimately determines our time on the earth (Job 14:5). Yet a life influenced by God's wisdom will help to lengthen life:

> Listen my son, accept what I say, and the years of your life will be many. *Proverbs 4:10*

> The fear of the Lord is the beginning of wisdom, and the knowledge of the Holy One is understanding. For by me your days will be multiplied, and years of life will be added to you. *Proverbs 9:10-11, NASB*

> The fear of the Lord prolongs life, but the years of the wicked will be shortened. *Proverbs 10:27, NASB*

Elderly saints were regarded as an asset to society:

> The righteous man will flourish like the palm tree, he will grow like a cedar in Lebanon. Planted in the house of the Lord, they will flourish in the courts of our God. They will still yield fruit in old age; they shall be full of sap and very green, to declare that the Lord is upright; He is my rock, and there is no unrighteousness in Him. *Psalm 92:12-15, NASB*

Not only did the righteous covet a good long life, God promised care for those whom he had brought to that stage.

Length of present life is indeed a proof of God's benevolence toward us.—*John Calvin*, Institutes

Listen to Me, O house of Jacob, and all the remnant of the house of Israel, you who have been borne by Me from birth, and have been carried from the womb; even to your old age, I shall be the same, and even to your graying years I shall bear you! I have done it, and I shall carry you; and I shall bear you, and I shall deliver you. *Isaiah 46:3-4*, NASB

A biblical perspective on life is not that we *get* old, not even that we *grow* old—both of these can be depressing—but that we *go* or die old, and that calls attention to God's goodness. It confirms God's gifting and guidance right up to departure time.

His work my hoary age shall bless
When youthful vigor is no more;
And my last hour of life confess
His saving love, his glorious power.
—*Philip Doddridge*

God-given bodies, managed in God-honoring activities, with sensible exercise, proper diet, and measured recreation, go a long way to promote and prolong life.

Adding Life to Years

Our grip on God can become firmer and stronger in proportion to the time we meditate on Scripture and pray. Faith muscles are exercised by such activities. Through Bible reading and prayer our faith is flexed, trimmed, and retrained. Adding years to life accompanies adding life to years. Bible reading promotes both.

Deep within us is a desire to know God better. Bible reading, prayer, and worship help to shape and sharpen that awareness. To deepen life is to lengthen it. Christian seniors have found reasons to live beyond statistical averages. When God adds to our years, we can use our influence for the sake of the gospel.

> Lord, it belongs not to my care
> Whether I die or live;
> To love and serve Thee is my share,
> And this Thy grace must give.
> If life be long, I will be glad
> That I may still obey;
> If short, yet why should I be sad
> To soar to endless day?
> —*Richard Baxter*

The illusion of avoiding old age

Society gears its advertising blitz, season after season, to deny and dodge aging. The expensive prescription cream Retin-A (Isotretinoin) does smooth wrinkles somewhat, but other creams that promise the disappearance of skin creases are fake cures. The cult of self captivates us and subtly convinces us to buy its products—lotions to grow new hair, rinses that restore old color, powders that soften the skin. Panicky people spend large amounts of money each year to look better, younger, and healthier. The best way to slow aging is to keep ourselves fit in the first place.

Probably the grossest extension of the secular illusion of never growing old is perpetuated by mind-control philosophies. New Age writer Linda Goodman, for instance, writes, "If you're eighty, you must learn how to reverse aging, in order to conquer disease and death."[12] Thinking young, blocking out death, determining to reverse aging will not stop anyone from dying, although the right mental attitude toward life and history go a long way to prolong and enrich our lives.

Psychic concentration attributes the power of longevity to people rather than to God. Mental determination and meditation methods exalt man as his own god. Christians find this emphasis to be a clear violation of the biblical understanding of human beings.

Scripture gives pointers on how to live long. Yet it stresses that God individualizes our history here as much as our destinies later. The Bible doesn't teach that the mind can stop or reverse aging. Moral and spiritual factors can lengthen life and enliven us, but positive outlooks will not keep us from leaving life in the normal way.

Prayer is an exercise of the mind and spirit. It is not mind control but a submission of our minds to the presence and will of God. Chanting stilted, disjointed mantras is not the way to build spiritual stamina. We have God's sure promises that unlock a future. It is not so much our prayers that produce results as God who responds to our articulated requests as we submit them to his final will.

Praying is an activity open to all seniors. Though aging is a process of giving up responsibilities to others, seniors still have burdens to unload on One who is greater than they. Through prayer we are either enabled to carry old or new burdens, or to cast them upon the Lord.

The elderly are often pictured in rockers. A rocker is the perfect choice for someone who wants to move while staying in one place! Yet a rocker requires some effort from the person who sits in it; a perfectly balanced rocker merely assists the user.

In the same way, our prayer lives need assistance sometimes. We want to pray, but our own "spontaneous" prayers don't seem to have enough energy of their own. At times like these, prayers written by others, whether in Scripture, prayer books, or some devotional material, can assist our conversations with God. Weak spiritual muscles need to be strengthened, not abandoned.

We can pray to live longer (King Hezekiah did: Isaiah 38), but God's prerogative may be to let us experience poor health and die sooner than we would like. Even in our pain we can find that God's mercies are fresh like the dawn and new each morning (Lamentations 3:22-23). The span of a life may be no longer than a handbreadth (Psalm 39:5), yet one person's span differs from another's.

Chapters 3 through 14 of this book are about seniors in the Bible. Each gave witness, directly or indirectly, to God's grace. In their responses to circumstances we find principles about how to react to temptations, tensions, burdens, transitions, and trials. From biblical characters we can learn what to seek and what to avoid, what makes for satisfaction and what contributes to misery.

But before we turn to examine individual seniors, we must wonder why God took the trouble to give lists of long-living people. Many a Bible reader has wondered why those long geneologies are in there! That is the subject of Chapter Two.

Wisdom does us no good if we don't apply it. At the end of each chapter are questions that will help you "put a handle" on what you're learning.

Things to think about:

1. How are *you* aging? Do you try to hide it?

2. This chapter discussed how laughter, mellowness, and spiritual calm add to a person's life. How do you rate in these areas?

3. Is mellowing an early stage of senility or a sign of maturity? How does a Christian who mellows with age differ from a non-Christian who mellows with age?

2

Biblical Records of Long Life

While biblical chronology is only approximately,
not mathematically accurate, it does not follow that
it is erroneous. There can be no mathematically
exact chronology. . . . Scripture chronology is free
from the fatally damaging error which characterizes
all the early ethnical chronology—namely, of attributing
an immense antiquity to man and nations.
W. G. T. SHEDD, *Dogmatic Theology*

The aging process could be delayed
if it had to make its way through Congress.
PRES. GEORGE BUSH,
State of Union Address, 1-28-92

CENTENARIANS (ANYONE 100 YRS. OLD OR OLDER) HAD SEMI-
celebrity status even in Old Testament times. While not
every centenarian was placed in Old Testament
genealogies, many otherwise forgotten seniors were
honored by being named in the abbreviated biblical
genealogies.

We know genealogies as "family trees." Many listed in
the biblical "family trees" lived astonishingly long. But
don't think you can pluck secrets on how to live long
from the branches of Old Testament genealogies.

Why, then, are genealogies included in Scripture?

Why Genealogies?

Genealogies act like wake-up alarms. They can turn us on, not off, to life, for genealogies are much more than lists of the dead and gone. They are celebrations of those still loved by God, who were major influences in this life and have moved on to eternal life.

The Old Testament, more than the New, carries its genealogies prominently and proudly. The impact of a life is partly in its length, for the longer one lives the more opportunities there are for affecting other lives.

Bible genealogies tell us how long some people lived, lining up forgotten ancestors as so many gold ingots in a bank vault. But in our speedy Alka-Seltzer age, we get bored with long directions, with long words, and with long genealogical lists!

Mormons, however, learn early to be genealogy buffs. More than that, Mormonism has made genealogical research a business, a ten-million-dollars-a-year business. Blasted out of the granite of the Wasatch Range in Utah, above the mouth of Little Cottonwood Canyon, are massive vaults protected by nine-ton metal doors and closed-circuit-television monitors. Deep in Utah over eighty workers tend with care and precision the records—primarily, of Mormons.

Mormons contend that genealogies are indispensable to salvation. Old Testament Jews were just as serious about record keeping but for different reasons. The issue was not the redemption of the dead, but the celebration of the living. The Jewish chroniclers provided lists of ancestors not because they needed saving but because they were agents of God's ongoing saving purposes. Tracing ancestors had value to the Hebrews, for God's promises were given through sets of individuals, tribes, and families. Some Old Testament genealogies are provided for historical perspective, and all were intentionally abbreviated.

Gaps, not gaffs, in genealogies

Gaps appear in Old Testament lists. Archbishop James Ussher's famous chronological calculations about the age of the earth (creation at 4004 B.C.) based on Old Testament archaeological and genealogical lists were inaccurate because he failed to factor in significant omissions.[1]

Bible genealogies were trimmed and tailored. Perhaps the most famous example is the genealogy of Jesus found in the first chapter of the book of Matthew.

Matthew's genealogy is divided into three segments of fourteen generations each. These divisions had Messianic clout, rather than giving simple sequence. The significance of three sets of doubled sevens symbolized the doubly perfect tri-unified Davidic line of the Messiah. (Also, there were redemptive and missiological reasons that four women—Tamar, Rahab, Ruth, and Bathsheba— were listed.) God rebuked cultural and chromosomal over-scrupulosity by their inclusion, for the four women were "outsiders."

Sometimes round numbers were given in place of exact figures. In Acts 7:6, Stephen was content to let "four hundred years" stick in the hearers' minds rather than the actual figure of 430.

Sometimes the description of a person's origin held more importance than the length of his or her life. Included in some genealogies are people who did not live particularly long lives. These insertions provide variety and remind us not to pass over biblical genealogies, for the lists are more than the record of the dead; *relationships* are also recorded. Occasionally, too, the standard genealogical formula was abandoned, such as the places where a confirmation of an answered prayer was inserted or when an incident of outstanding heroism was recorded (such as 1 Chronicles 4:10).

One function of biblical genealogies was to remind the nation in subsequent generations that little people mattered, that their sacrifices did not go unnoticed by God. God notices individuals. He does not forget names or fumble around to fix identities.

> Can a woman forget her nursing child, and not have compassion on the son of her womb? Surely they may forget, yet I will not forget you. See, I have inscribed you on the palms of My hands; your walls are continually before Me. *Isaiah 49:15-16, NKJV*

The third most popular hobby in the U.S. (behind stamp and coin collecting) is genealogical research. Whereas in 1966 there were only two hundred genealogical organizations, today they number over eight hundred. Nevertheless, most Christians are tempted to skip the Bible's genealogical chapters. Some may think God concocted genealogies to bore us.

To the Jews, however, genealogies represented the importance of their own heritage. They were a people with a history—as tangible as those written words. Hebrew parents may have insisted that their children not skip reading them—possibly to impress upon them the importance of marrying within their own race and culture.

A reporter asked a 105-year-old man about his secret for living long. He replied, "Don't know for certain yet. My lawyer is negotiating with two breakfast food companies!"

The esteemed psychiatrist, the late Paul Tournier, was up-front in confessing his youthful disinterest in biblical genealogies:

When I was young I used to think that [Bible genealogies] could well have been dropped from the Biblical canon. But I have since realized that their series of proper names bear witness to the fact that, in the biblical perspective, man is neither a thing nor an abstraction, neither a species nor an idea, that he is not a fraction of the mass, as the Marxists see him, but that he is a person.[2]

Biblical "family trees" have been regarded by some as a preliminary print-out of the guest list for heaven's final celebrations. That appears to have been the conclusion of an elderly Christian woman who was asked why she did not skip over the first nine chapters of Chronicles (solid with genealogical files) but read them all. She said, "I would feel dreadful if I got to heaven and met those people and didn't know their names." (The dear saint was too generous, for in the scales of spiritual realism it is too optimistic to imagine that all those in the Chronicles lists would be in heaven!)

Surprises in genealogies
Genealogies sit in Scripture, not like bobbing corks on an inland lake but like fallen logs across a mountain road. They are there to slow us up and to get us to think about the role of real people in the progress of redemption. On the other hand, making too much of ancestors may draw attention away from the ageless God and Creator, whose goodness best accounts for the blessings we enjoy—including long life. Our ties in the present are surely in-

fluenced by past links, but our past is less important than
the God who occupies our past, present, and future.

People are not saved or heaven-bound because of their
ancestral roots. How many times have people felt more
pious than others because they have had so many
preachers in the family! That we descended from great
orators or great Christian leaders is of little consequence.
God, in one sense, doesn't care whether you are a de-
scendant of Jonathan Edwards or Genghis Khan. He
does immensely care, however, what your relationship is
to Jesus Christ. Sifting through our past for sterling characters may yield a few nugget-level Christians, but
having them as part of our heritage will not inch us
closer to heaven. Christian relatives do not make us
Christians. The question is not who we know, or who
we're related to, but our connection with Christ.

Ironically, those most proud of their ancestral ties were
Jesus' most vehement opponents. The Pharisees made a big
deal about their Abraham connection, about their Jewish-
ness. Every Jew had the claim to one famous ancestor:
Abraham. But while Abraham is justly lauded as a man of
faith, God looked for faith *like* that of Abraham, not faith *in*
Abraham. In fact, to those with an Abraham-fixation, Jesus
said in essence, "Your father is the Devil!" (John 8:44).

Bible readers know that two of the Gospels begin with
Jesus' genealogies. Matthew focused on Jesus belonging
to the proper race for Messianic fulfillment, because
Joseph, Jesus' foster-father, descended from David. Luke
tells us that Mary was the legitimate bearer of the Messiah because she also descended from David.

A Biblical Roster of Old "Roosters"

Genesis 5 has more old men bunched together than
anywhere else in the Bible. Seven of the ten were over
nine hundred years old! They are centuries apart from

other biblical ancients, even older than the three major Hebrew patriarchs: Abraham who lived to be 175, Isaac who reached 180, and Jacob who left life at 147.

We have kindly called the men of Genesis 5 "roosters." Skeptics have often questioned the accuracy of the years listed in Genesis 5. Could anyone have lived so long? The assumption is that no one could have lived the phenomenal ages claimed for the ten patriarchs.

1. Adam lived 930 years.
2. Seth lived 912 years.
3. Enosh lived 905 years.
4. Kenan or Cainan lived 910 years.
5. Mahahalalel lived 895 years.
6. Jared lived 962 years.
7. Enoch lived 365 years—but he left early (Genesis 5:24)!
8. Methuselah lived 969 years.
9. Lamech lived 777 years.
10. Noah lived 950 years.

Two additional features of this list also stand out.

*Their fertility was as amazing as their age. Seth fathered Enosh at age 105, for instance.

*Seven out of ten lived over nine hundred years. Enoch could have lived past nine hundred also, but God took him alive to heaven.

The patriarchs lived centuries, then
God shortened the lifespan of men;
And so, to conform
To the Biblical norm,
He kept us to "threescore and ten."
—D. R. Benson, adapted by the author

How does one account for those record ages? Too many write off this genealogy as sheer fantasy. We don't have the space to examine all the explanations that might account for these pre-Flood ancients. But I will briefly sketch the main explanations so you can pursue the matter further if you wish.

Theological explanation

Some have appealed to the purity of the human race as a major factor in pre-Flood longevity. Soon after the Fall of humankind, diseases were fewer, viruses were less potent, and the human body was stronger (than now). Germ mutations had not yet accelerated, and perhaps there was less contamination from nature.

Semantic explanation

Debates among Old Testament experts as to whether "years" meant years as we know them or whether they were a literary device (or both) cannot be considered here. A preliminary debate on these matters can be found in the pro/con book, *The Genesis Debate* (1986), edited by Ronald Youngblood, in Chapter 8, "The Ages of Those Before the Flood."[3]

Without denying historicity, it is not entirely farfetched to argue that symbolism was intended in early Genesis. The NIV Study Bible's note on Genesis 5:5 reads:

> Enoch's 365 (v. 23) years (365 being the number of days in a year, thus a full life) and Lamech's 777 (v. 31) years (777 being an expansion and multiple of seven, the number of completeness; cf. The "seventy-seven times" of Lamech's namesake in 4:24). The fact that there are ten names in the Genesis 5 list (as in the genealogy of 11:10-26) makes it likely that it includes gaps, the lengths of which may be summarized in the

large numbers. Other ancient genealogies outside the Bible exhibit similarly large figures.

Environmental explanation
One interesting hypothesis for explaining the enormous ages of the pre-Flood people is the state of meteorological conditions. This view holds that the pre-Flood generations benefited from a vapor canopy that moistened the earth and protected life from the sun (Genesis 1:6-8).

A vast water canopy, goes the reasoning, enveloped the earth. Rain did not water the earth until the time of the Flood. The density of the canopy accounts for the copious water in the forty-day rain that produced the Flood.[4]

The moisture shield provided a protective ceiling for humans. A semitropical atmosphere, along with a heavily moistured covering, screened out cosmic radiation and contributed to longer life.

The plausibility of this idea has been vigorously and comprehensively treated in a long book, *The Waters Above.*[5] The subject is enormously fascinating and Dillow's treatment of it brings together significant scientific, grammatic, and historic reasoning.

What about the Future?

Do we not insult divine intelligence to contend there must be literal accounting books in heaven? Would there be any need or value in having a directory, such as those phone companies compile on earth? Does perfection of knowledge do away with lists?

Final answers are not available on these matters. But Revelation is understandable to us because record keeping is pictured to us as continuing in the hereafter. God not only made us one by one, but those who enter heaven are counted. Revelation uses specific large numbers to describe heaven's population, not in a literal sense but to show its magnitude. Those who enter the final heaven will not sneak in. Revelation 21:27 reminds us that God has a security check at the Pearly Gates. Excluded from entrance are those who are secretly but significantly wicked. Not only is the population of heaven stable, its records are partly statistical.

Despite the heavy emphasis on record keeping in the Bible, there is a central passage that is one clear instance of God scorning genealogies! Amazingly, Jesus, one of whose titles is "high priest," had no genealogical record to warrant his wearing that title! Jesus was priest, but one could not look him up in the Levite family tree. The Levite tribe was specified as the tribe from which Israel's priests would come; yet Jesus did not come from the line of Levi. But he was God's final and highest priest.

For high priesthood, Jesus' claim was that of the line of Melchizedek. For that line a genealogical record was meaningless. Hebrews 7:3 points out that the absence of genealogical records on Melchizedek did not diminish or put to question Jesus' right to be high priest. Christ was not an Aaronic priest. Unlike any Aaronic priest Christ was a perpetual high priest because of his indestructible life (Hebrews 7:16).

Today, seeing names on a genealogical chart should stimulate our appreciation of the diversity of our origins. If for no other reason, biblical genealogies confirm that the participants in God's redemptive history were real people.

But life is more than lists of names. People are more precious than records, charts, and photocopies of baptismal documents. And the point of living is not to get special mention in a family history, regional history, state history, or even national history.

Clearly, living a godly life brings more satisfaction than seeing our name or the names of relatives in paper files. The lives of seniors in the Old and New Testaments will inspire us to live out our lives completely for the glory of God.

Things to think about:

1. What might you miss by skipping over the genealogies of Scripture? By doing that, are you slighting its authority?

2. Does it bother you that the biblical genealogies include mostly men? (After all, it's women who have the babies!) Who are the four women listed in Matthew's genealogy of Jesus? Why were they included?

3. Think about your spiritual heritage. What qualities in the lives of people in your family's past generations have made it easier to follow the Christian way? What qualities have made following Christ more difficult?

3

Job: A Senior Who Confessed in Print

In the play *JB*, Nickles throws in his two cents
(speaking for Satan):
You know what talks when that man's talking?
All that gravy on his plate—
His cash—his pretty wife—his children!
Lift the lot of them, he'd sing
Another canticle to different music.
ARCHIBALD MACLEISH, *JB*

IF THERE WERE A BIBLICAL HALL OF FAME, JOB WOULD BE featured as the senior who wrote the first "tell-all" autobiography. The virtuosity of the book reflects the vitality of the man.

Job's autobiography was a long poem, an epic by an epochal man. He was out to teach rather than titillate in "tell-all" fashion. According to essayist Thomas Carlyle, Job is "the most wonderful poem of any age and language." Archibald MacLeish wrote his Pulitzer Prize-winning play, *JB*, based on the original masterpiece.

Job skillfully arrayed an armada of animals to shoot down dive-bombing cynics. Especially beautiful are his descriptions of wild donkeys (39:5-12), the ostrich (39:13-18), the horse (39:19-25), and birds of prey (39:26-30). Nowhere else in Scripture can one find such a detailed description of the leviathan or crocodile (41:1-34). But Job is far more than a nature handbook. *National Geographic* video lovers meet spiritual realities in this book.

Job's love for God was severely tested. His troubles were not the result of random forces in nature, but the playing out of God's will. In Chapter 1 of Job, Satan and God went at it, tooth and nail, in bracing dialogue. Satan wanted God to shuffle Job's fortunes, rather than simply wait to see Job shuffle his feet in simpering old age.

To Satan, Job was little more than an experimental human and God no greater than a fellow lab partner. God let Lucifer harangue. He even allowed him to slice Job in different ways and to put him on slides for everyone to see. But he refused to concede that Job was a mere specimen for a celestial pathologist. The ultimate lesson of the book was not the virtue of Job, but God's absolute justice and sovereignty.

Three so-called friends (Eliphaz, Bildad, Sophar) jabbered at Job. Elihu described them as "aged" (32:6, NRSV). But the advice of the senior threesome proved arid and hollow, reminding us that not every elder gives dependable wisdom.

Spread out over Job's ponderous pages are both derogatory and complimentary perceptions of God. Job himself was not so hot a theologian, nor so skilled a debater. Calvin correctly noted that Job had "a good case [but] pleads it poorly, and [his three cynical friends had] a poor case [but] plead it well."[1]

Job, however, grew in his understanding of God as the book progressed. By the second half of the book, and especially in the conclusion, Job confessed that it was dishonoring to think of God as his personal servant. God spoke directly to Job near the end of the book, and Job repented of his small view of God's sovereignty.

Yet even in some of the earlier sections praise of God shines through. Job 1:21 is a powerful affirmation of God: "The LORD gave and the LORD has taken away, may the name of the LORD be praised."

Yet Job knew frustration, too. When his eyes faced the blur of a weaver's shuttle, he confessed, "My days are swifter than a weaver's shuttle" (Job 7:6). This instrument had blazing speed. In its rapid, relentless, and repetitive motion Job saw an illustration of his short life whizzing by.

Even at that, Job was an optimist in disguise, for instead of viewing God as unraveling him, eventually he saw the Almighty working through him. God works out his purposes through his people, however short or long their lives. King Hezekiah approximated Job's imagery when he said on his death bed, "Like a weaver I have rolled up my life, and he has cut me off from the loom; day and night you made an end of me" (Isaiah 38:12).

"My days are swifter than a weaver's shuttle." In that statement Job reflected some frustration with life. Before we express a breezy optimism or lift our noses to sniff out new challenges, we, too, must get ready to face life's limitations. In early adulthood we say "Why not!" whereas some seniors are overheard to ask "Why bother?" Someone described the senior years as taking longer and longer to do less and less.

Acknowledging human brevity is healthy. We do that best, like Job, by recognizing God as our security in life's passages. Anxieties and apprehensions about time's ravages become less inhibiting, frustrating, and self-destructive when we lay them before God.

Life's Proportions

A number of years ago Westinghouse washers used the slogan, "After it spins dry, it shuts off automatically."

(Some wish preachers would operate the same way!) But the idea of shutting off automatically pre-dates modern washing machines. Job could say the same thing about leg-pumped looms. After they run out of thread, there is no sense in continued pumping.

Looms work off spools. Each spool contains so many yards of thread. God has given us so many days. Life, as we know it, will run out. The day comes when speed stops and there is no more spiel on our spool. Each year is like a yard of rope or thread. When the thread God allows us runs out, the loom stops. Life on earth comes to a halt when God calls us home.

Some seniors are given large spools. *The American Baptist* magazine issue for September, 1991 honored the Reverend Johnson, age ninety-one, still preaching at his church in Chicago. The *Sunday Digest* carried my article on a retired Lutheran minister of Worland, Wyoming. Throughout his seventies and eighties Dr. Berkenkamp earned mega-thousands of dollars for world missions through his rock-pot project.[2]

"How near the end of the spool are we?" We have all wondered when our earthly lives will run out. Sometimes the thread of life runs out before seventy. With others, due to crib death, an accident, unexpected cancer, or a viral infection, a person's life line is snapped early.

We waste time speculating how long we will contribute to the fabric of society. Science has shown that there is not just one spool feeding thread into our life's machine. I thought of this when I had a tour of the Morgan Knitting Mills of Pennsylvania, where waffle-weave underwear was first made and is still manufactured. It is one of three major mills that supply waffle cloth to many winter underwear manufacturers.

I was given the tour by the inventor of the waffle-weave machine, Mr. Alvin Ditzler. He explained that typical machines weaving this type of cloth have 800 to

1,000 needles and are fed by eight to ten spools. When the thread runs out, it does so (as you may guess) in stages—a spool at a time. Human life is like that. Our bodies wear out in stages. For some, the eyesight or memory weakens first; for others the problems are with blood, vital organs, bones and joints, or hormones/emotions. We "run down" before we "run out" of life.

Life's Pattern

In a sense, a woman's womb is where bodies and souls are woven. Each person is individually made; each pattern is unique. The mills of God may work exceedingly slow, but they work exceedingly fine. We reflect God's weaving, emerging with distinctive colors and patterns. Some lives wear well and last long. Others can't bear the stress. They snap with their spool half used. Long life is not simply the working out of natural law in conformity with a genetic code. It comes down to the author, organizer, and dispenser of the thread of life: God. In Proverbs 9:11 he says, "Through me your days will be many." Unlike cloth or carpet, our life patterns may switch threads in midcourse. Unexpected changes can tie us up in knots and hasten our end. How we turn out and what God designs for us is purposefully and completely hidden from us.

Go back with me, briefly, to the knitting factory tour, where I saw the waffle machines pouring out long sheets of soon-to-warm, soon-to-be-worn undercloth. Mr. Ditzler pointed out that the seemingly simple weave machine has produced 1,886 styles since its first running in 1949. The weave-pattern underwear comes from the program supplied to it by a hidden cam. The cam, a circular disk larger and heavier than the human hand, dictates every part of each pattern. There may be as many as sixteen spools on the more advanced machines and 1,800 or more needles, but it is the cam that guarantees the design and its flawless duplication.

Similarly, we are born with God-designed, God implanted, God-maintained cams inside us. Scientists tell us that genetic information is stored in our chromosomes. What we are yet to be, as well as what we are, is stored in a molecule called DNA. The DNA contains the human genes, which are the basic units of heredity. Job said it in nontechnical and prescientific form:

> Man's days are determined; you have decreed the number of months and have set limits he cannot exceed. 14:5

Too often we linger over our life's pattern, pondering to the point of paralysis the future and how productive we will or will not be. Predictability is not a plus; actually, it can take away from the quality of our lives. If we know the bad, we can become terrified. If we know what is good, we may feel complacent or conceited. The main thing is that we get our lives in line with God's Word, which gives instruction on how to live well. Trying to discern the ultimate design is defeating, for

> We see a few loose threads on the back side of life's tapestry, and unless we are told by the weaver, we can only guess at the shape of the future.[3]

For Job it was enough to be impressed with the shuttle's speed. He did not bother to investigate the weaver's pattern. He was right, for that is God's prerogative. Isaiah 55:8 reinforces the need for us to stay clear of probing God's secret decrees: "My thoughts are not your thoughts, neither are your ways my ways, says the Lord." The Hebrew word for "thoughts" is, literally, "weavings." The root of the word means "mingling threads of different colors."[4]

Who we are and where we are is God's business. We belong to him. We could not, nor should we, try to calculate our lives. If we knew, our natures would tend to focus on the dark threads. *God's brightest designs and most beautiful patterns go unappreciated because our anticipations are too rigid.*

Samuel Rutherford, a Scots Presbyterian of the 1600s, could have avoided pain and imprisonment if he had compromised his views of the church. But he saw the need to stand for principles that went to the very heart of the church's future. In his famous hymn, "Immanuel's Land," he commented on his checkered career:

> With mercy and with judgment
> My web of life He wove,
> And aye, the dews of sorrow
> Were lustred with His love;
> I'll bless the hand that guided
> I'll bless the heart that planned,
> When throned where glory dwelleth
> In Immanuel's land.
> —*Samuel Rutherford*

I like the words, "Our life is like the weaver's web," for it is so true to life. We only see the wrong side of the fabric now, for the Weaver has not finished his work. But in the Day to come, where we shall see it from his side, then we shall behold the beauty of his work and not the knots and ends which our sins and failures have caused.—*Vera Pink*

Each of us has a future perfectly planned by God. The form and final design are out of our hands, though God works through the work of *our* hands. It is enough for us to trust our lives to him.

My life is but a weaving
Between my Lord and me,
I cannot choose the colors
He worketh steadily.
Oftimes He weaveth sorrow,
And I in foolish pride
Forget He sees the upper
And I, the underside.
Not till the loom is silent
And the shuttles cease to fly
Shall God unroll the canvas
And explain the reason why.
The dark threads are as needful
In the weaver's skillful hand
As the threads of gold and silver
In the pattern He has planned.
—*Grant Colfax Tullar*

Things to think about:

1. Does your life seem to be moving slowly or quickly? What affects how fast the time goes for you?

2. Think of several difficult times in your life. What good did God work out for you?

3. Why do we think that—even at a distance—we can discern an overall pattern to life?

4

Abraham: A Senior Who Trusted God's Abundance

At Moriah God tried Abraham to see
if he believed in God enough to sacrifice his son.
On Calvary, God tries you and me, to see if we have
faith enough in God to believe that he loves us
enough to sacrifice his own Son.
CLARENCE E. MACARTNEY

DIANE SAWYER INTERVIEWED SEVERAL PEOPLE IN THEIR nineties on a segment of ABC News "PrimeTime Live." In her summary she said, "In the future, for more and more people, the nineties will be as vital and creative as middle age. The nineties could be the best years of your life."[1]

Did you ever notice that God often entrusted leadership to oldtimers at key turning points? Often their greatest works were done in their latter years! Moses lived to be 120 years. His first forty years were preparation years. The second forty were spent in the desert tending sheep. It was only in his last forty years that his greatest achievements came!

Abraham was old when he began a nation. Moses was old when he led the nation. Although Abraham was probably Israel's most illustrious senior, Moses was probably its most industrious leader. God didn't give either one of them "incentives" to take early retirement. Younger men were available, but God chose these two seniors at pivotal points in Old Testament history to achieve his ends.

The American Association of Retired People is thirty-three million strong. AARP packs enormous power as a Washington, D.C. lobby. AARP would (if they could) have made room for Abraham and Moses on their Advisory Board. But how could Moses and Abraham qualify since neither of them ever retired! Both patriarchs worked till they dropped.

Business minds realize that age is no detriment to productive labor. That is why they seek the skills of such men as Armand Hammer who headed Occidental petroleum into his eighties. John F. Connelly, president of Philadelphia-based Crown Cork and Seal, Inc., still guided the company with steady hand at age seventy-five. Oldsters don't just blow off steam, they bubble with enterprising management ideas and stimulate better products.

Counted as Righteous, God's Friend

Abram (we'll call him Abraham, as God later renamed him) was called out of paganism to be a believer in the one true God. Jehoshaphat, Isaiah, and James called Abraham "God's Friend" (2 Chronicles 20:7; Isaiah 41:8; James 2:23). The author of Hebrews celebrated Abraham's faith in obeying God's call for him to leave Ur of the Chaldees (11:8-10). Even in Islam Abraham is called "The Bosom Friend of Allah."

Celebrated for his loyalty, affection, and dedication, on one point he seemed an absolute failure. Though he was industrious and wealthy (in the world of shepherds), when it came to fathering a male successor, a son to be heir, he was a washout. By the time Abraham was in his eighties and Sarah in her seventies, they both seemed to have lost out on parenthood.

Abraham was a disappointed senior. He battled the same inner conflicts between his desire to have and God's design to produce. Abraham and Sarah were to produce a son but at a time when God chose.

Inexperienced faith

Abraham had been in a hurry to have a son. But he wasn't in that much of a hurry to trust God completely. He didn't exercise enough faith in God to wave off Sarah's insistence that he father a son through Hagar and thereby get a male heir in a manner God had not chosen. He was in a rush to get an answer.

Abraham gave God a few years to deliver on his promise. After that, he said in effect, "OK, God; time's up." Hagar became a substitute, surrogate spouse. Abraham's impatience with God led to the use of Hagar. But their son Ishmael was not the son of promise.

God reappeared to Abraham thirteen years after Ishmael was born.

> **W**hen Abram was ninety-nine years old, the LORD [Jehovah] appeared to him and said, "I am God Almighty [El Shaddai], walk before me and be blameless. I will confirm my covenant between me and you and will greatly increase your numbers."
> *Genesis 17:1*

God wanted Abraham to know he was *El Shaddai*. Each name of God in the Old Testament emphasized a different facet of God's nature. *Yahweh*, (Jehovah) emphasized God's covenant-keeping nature. This is the first place in the Bible where God as El Shaddai appears.

El Shaddai emphasized God's fullness, abundance, and richness. He is God the all-sufficient One, the God who is more than enough. Philologist Robert B. Girdlestone says, "The name *El* sets forth the might of God, the title *Shaddai* points to the inexhaustible stores of His bounty."[2]

It is important to note that at this stage of Abraham's life he was already declared righteous. He had thrown his life into the lap of God earlier when God called him out of Ur of the Chaldees. Abraham trusted his life completely to the only true God and thus was declared righteous (Genesis 15:6).

However, Abraham was more eager to have a son than to acquire real estate. Possessing Canaan wasn't Abraham's passion, because he was looking for a heavenly city. (See Hebrews 11:12-16.)

Did God promise the patriarch merely an earthly acquisition? If so, subsequent events have clearly shown that the promise has not been kept. It cannot be disputed that the country of Canaan has not been an everlasting possession either of Abraham or of his seed: at best, they have only enjoyed a footing in this land at intermittent intervals; and for a period of approximately eighteen hundred years since the final anti-Roman revolt under Bar-Cochla this territory has been the possession of Gentile people.[3]

Could God be trusted when neither land nor son could be seen? That was Abraham's test. Reliance on God alone was Abraham's greatest challenge. He came to the point where he trusted the Lord fully, and so became an example of complete faith in God's righteousness alone (Romans 4:1-13).

God's trustworthiness, not ours

Abraham showed faltering faith at times, but he was not unjustified by his missteps. His salvation was not reversed by his lapse. His choice to use Hagar did not cancel Abraham's acceptance by God, because the bottom line for salvation is *God's* truthfulness rather than *our* trustworthiness.

Martin Luther, as a young priest, realized that self-cleansings showed only partial trust in God's Son as Savior. He saw he could not do enough, repent enough, or pray enough. His problem was that *he* was trying to be enough rather than trusting in God's abundance.

John Bunyan didn't know a thankful heart until he trusted his salvation completely to Jesus Christ. In his autobiography, *Grace Abounding,* he wrote:

> I . . . saw . . . that it was not my good frame of heart that made my righteousness better, nor yet my bad frame that made my righteousness worse, for my righteousness was Jesus Christ Himself . . . Now Christ was all: all my righteousness, all my sanctification, and all my redemption.[4]

Outside Madrid, Spain, there is a famed ancient monastery where the kings of Spain have been buried. The church is a magnificent example of architectural beauty. The architect designed an elongated arch so flat that it frightened the king who inspected the work. The king did not think that the arch would hold the weight of the upper structure, so he ordered the architect to add a column to buttress what was already there. The architect insisted that it was unnecessary, but the king prevailed. The column was built as ordered.

Years later the king died and was buried in the church with the other Spanish kings. Then the architect revealed that the column was made a quarter of an inch short of the arch. And in the intervening years the arch never sagged in the slightest.

Similarly, the finished work of Christ and his righteousness cannot be improved upon. It does not need an added support, the addition of our contributions. We dishonor the architect of our salvation to try to shore up the perfect redemption of Christ.

> Enough for me that Jesus saves,
> This ends my fear and doubt;
> A sinful soul I come to Him,
> He'll never cast me out.
> I need no other argument,
> I need no other plea,
> It is enough that Jesus died,
> And that He died for me.
> —L. H. Edmunds

Abraham's Supreme Failure

Abraham was a justified man when God appeared to him as El Shaddai, the God of good and plenty, the all-sufficient, powerful God. He was accepted by God as righteous, but Abraham had not yet fully trusted in God's timetable.

The physical obstacles of his age—Abraham was ninety-nine and Sarah was eighty-nine—took his attention away from the opportunities God could create. While thinking of his deficiencies he took his eyes off God's all-sufficiency.

Abraham looked at what he didn't have, not on the God who promised a son in their old age. Abraham did not thank God enough for being God. He was thankful for his financial blessings, for his health, and for his acceptance by God. But Abraham had fallen down in trusting God for doing the humanly impossible.

Lack of gratitude for mercies received was not Abraham's problem. He was a thankful man. His difficulty was in trusting God for a male heir. The answer would not be found in what Abraham did or who he was, but in who God is.

Have we given up?

Few of us will reach our nineties, but most of us ask ourselves the question Abraham asked himself in his ninety-ninth year. We ask ourselves if God can do anything through us when we pass into old age. We get two answers: one from our bodies; the other from God. The answer from our bodies is that we are finished. But the answer from God is that he can accomplish his purposes through those who we and others think are washed up and worn out.

When we meditate on God our outlooks change about the potentialities ahead. We limit God to think that he uses only the vigorous and young. It is the vastness of God's power that explains how he can use and reuse the elderly.

Ralph Waldo Emerson told of an old woman "who had been pinched with poverty all her life." When she had her first boat ride on the ocean she stood and gazed. She gazed so long that people began to wonder if she was all right. When someone asked her what she was thinking about, she replied, "I'm so glad to see something at last that there is enough of." During World War II, a soldier from the Southwest U.S.A., one not used to seeing an ocean, marveled while on his transatlantic troop ship, "That's more water than I have ever seen in my entire life." Another soldier piped up, "You ain't seen nothin' yet. That's just the top of it."

> Thy goodness and Thy truth to me,
> To every soul, abound,
> A vast unfathomable sea,
> Whence all my thoughts are drowned.
> Its streams the whole creation reach,
> So plenteous is the store,
> Enough for all, enough for each,
> Enough for evermore.
> —*Charles Wesley*

When are we satisfied?

Abraham was rebuked for focusing on his infirmities when called to trust his life to God's immense power. We are, too. God's plenteous goodness and unwearied might are enough to challenge our minds, enough to fill and overflow our souls, enough to satisfy our needs, and enough to use and repay our labor. Paul discovered the secret when he wrote, "My God will meet all your needs, according to his glorious riches in Christ Jesus" (Philippians 4:19).

> His grace is great enough to meet the great things,
> The crashing waves that overwhelm the soul,
> The roaring winds that leave us stunned and breathless,
> The sudden storms beyond our life's control.
> His grace is great enough to meet the small things,
> The little pin-prick troubles that annoy,
> The insect worries, buzzing and persistent,
> The squeaking wheels that grate upon our joy.
> —*Unknown*

With God—El Shaddai—the God of good and plenty, nothing is impossible.

Say not, my soul, 'From whence can God relieve my care?'
Remember that Omnipotence has servants everywhere.
—*Unknown*

Having enough to live *on* has replaced the concern of having enough to live *for*. To Americans, *being* enough is not nearly as important as *having* enough.

We cannot read about Abraham or study the turning points of his life without our own faith being tested. Like Abraham we may find that full reliance upon God does not seem necessary until we have first encountered absolute failure. Abraham was able to trust God fully when he came to the end of himself. That is the point we must reach before our faith in the Lord becomes full.

We need to ask: Are we obsessed with achieving success so that we can rightly be proud? Do we desire strength merely to keep us active? Or are we eager to exercise great faith in God's grace so we have a healthy hope?

—— ♪ ——

Things to think about:

1. When pushed into a corner, do you become more focused on yourself (pity party) or on God's superabundance?

2. When have you been astonished by the abundance and righteousness of God? What effect did it have on your life?

3. What kind of timetables have you given God in which to accomplish certain things in your life?

5

Sarah: A Senior Whose Laughter Was Revealing

Sarah and her husband had had plenty of hard knocks
in their time, and there were plenty more of them
still to come, but at that moment
when the angel told them they'd better start
dipping into their old age pensions for cash
to build a nursery, the reason they laughed
was that it suddenly dawned upon them
that the wildest dreams they'd ever had
hadn't been half wild enough.
FREDERICK BUECHNER, *Peculiar Treasures*

Births are happy events. In my neighborhood colorful balloons are tied to posters on front lawns announcing—"It's a Boy!" or "It's a Girl!" Babies bring joy and the way they are born can make us laugh.

Once a grammar-school teacher assigned her class to write a brief essay on births in their families. One student did his homework by asking his father, "Where did I come from?" His father said, "The stork brought you."

"Where did *you* come from?" continued the little boy. "The stork brought me," his father replied.

"Where did *your* father come from?" the boy pressed. "The stork brought him, too," the father answered, exasperated.

The boy wrote his essay. The teacher was shocked to read his opening line: "There hasn't been a normal birth in our family for three generations."

Sometimes, however, reality can be funnier than fantasy. I mean no disrespect to women, for giving birth is no joke. But for a ninety-year-old woman to give birth is bizarre. Parenthood at one hundred and at ninety! What a shock! What a puzzle! It is one of the best-known, humorous Old Testament stories.

Appropriately, they named the boy "laughter" (we know him as "Isaac"). He was not called laughter because he looked funny. He was named "laughter" because his elderly parents giggled at the notice of his coming.

Sarah has the distinction of being the only senior in Scripture to be a first-time mother. It is a true story laced with laughter. Both parents laughed. But God had the last laugh in letting everyone else in on their story.

Why Did Sarah Laugh?

Sarah must have taken her physical appearance seriously. Her beauty was so transparent that it made status-conscious men willing to leap social barriers. She was desired by two different kings to be included in their harems, that of the Egyptian Pharaoh and of the Philistine Abimelech.

Let's not be prudish. Sarah was stunning, even sensual. She was stared at a-plenty. Old men gave her admiring glances and young men turned for a second look. Her hourglass figure hadn't lost a second. The Dead Sea Scrolls described Sarah as follows: "How fair indeed are her eyes and how pleasing her nose and all the radiance of her face . . . and how lovely all her whiteness . . . her arms how good to look upon, and her hands how perfect."[1]

Sarah undoubtedly handled her aging process heroically and creatively. She kept her beauty longer than most. A spot check of her travel luggage may have turned up something comparable to rose milk, perfume, eyebrow pencil, and rouge. But by age eighty-five, she probably had given away her box of baby powder and had sold her port-a-crib.

Sarah had made a difficult switch. Just think of it—she left a sumptuous home in Ur of Chaldees to bum around with Abraham for years in the desert. She exchanged a tile kitchen floor for basic sand. Sarah had true grit.

Sarah had to have a sense of humor to survive life in the desert. No matter how much one may appreciate beauty, tent-living could quickly make a beautiful woman sound like a grouch. But the sand did not turn Sarah sour.

Sarah's flip side, however, was not a laughing matter. She had a mean streak as well as a funny bone. One matter made her nasty. She respected her husband (1 Peter 3:6), but she showed revenge against Hagar, her servant who was contracted to be a surrogate mother when Sarah's infertility stretched into her eighties (Genesis 16:4-6).

Sarah had an egg-shell ego. She accused Hagar of contempt when she was the one who scorned Hagar's ability to give Abraham a child. She blamed Abraham, when it was she who could not admit to her own error in prematurely insisting that Hagar conceive a boy by Abraham.

Her impatience, according to some, would have knocked her out of Faith's Hall of Fame (Hebrews 11). If put to a vote, Hagar and Ishmael would have protested and picketed her inclusion. Whereas Abraham was magnanimous and conciliatory toward Hagar, Sarah became bitter and berating. What older woman wouldn't resent a younger one who could finally give her husband a child? And it didn't help that Hagar, once she knew she was pregnant, "despised" Sarah. Sarah's frosty disposition sent a chill through the tent of Abraham at high noon. Hagar's fertility drove Sarah to jealous anger so much so that "her husband had to bow his head beneath the blast, and her maid to flee into the wilderness."[2]

Sarah was eighty-nine when God informed Abraham that she would conceive within the year.

> Sarah was listening at the entrance to the tent . . . and laughed to herself as she thought, "After I am worn out and my master is old, will I now have this pleasure?"
>
> Then the LORD said to Abraham, "Why did Sarah laugh and say, 'Will I really have a child, now that I am old?' Is anything too hard for the LORD? I will return to you at the appointed time next year and Sarah will have a son."
>
> Sarah was afraid, so she lied and said, "I did not laugh."
>
> But he said, "Yes, you did laugh." *Genesis 18:10-15*

One day after kindergarten at Philadelphia's Northeast Christian School, we asked our daughter, Leslie, what she learned. She said, "God told Sarah she would have a baby 100 years old, and she laughed." That was one joke God did not pull on Sarah!

If Sarah had no sense of humor, she could not have laughed at God's birth notice. Yet there are many different shades of laughter. Was Sarah's laugh laced with disbelief or was it merely a rueful chuckle? Or was her laugh edged in bitter sarcasm? She undoubtedly felt that God was playing a joke on her. One can only imagine the pain she had borne during all those years over being childless; it would be safe to say that the laugh God overheard was laced with that pain—and possibly some anger at the many times her hopes for motherhood had been dashed.

At a time in Sarah's life when she would have expected to enter a peaceful old age, she was told that her life was about to be turned upside down with the hyperactive years of childcare. Imagine a person headed for the geriatric ward but ending up in the maternity ward! On the other hand, Abraham fell on his face in adoration; awe of God's presence overwhelmed him. Abraham was inclined to laugh at the possibility of fatherhood, but it was not a cynical laugh.

> Abraham's was a laugh of admiration and joy; Sarah's was a laugh of unbelief and distrust. . . . Abraham laughed because he believed it would be so, Sarah because she believed it could not be so.[3]

> Her laughter . . . was of contemptuous doubt, the laughter of Abraham that of delighted astonishment.[4]

That Sarah apparently muffled her laughter was not necessarily proof of her doubt.[5] Good manners could have caused her to cover her mouth. Sometimes we cover our mouth to hide the intensity of a laugh; even then some laughter was considered a social indiscretion.

Maybe Sarah was enjoying the irony of it all—the absurdity of being pregnant at ninety. Maybe she misheard. But we know it was not the first time she heard of her late-life expectancy. It was the fourth time that God said she would bear a boy in her old age. First, she doubted that God *would* do it. Finally, she doubted that God *could* do it.

Had not Sarah shown the extent of her doubt by arranging for Abraham to father a child through Hagar?

We know Sarah's laughter was edged in sarcasm, for her denial of having laughed showed that she knew she laughed cynically. Sarah unwisely thought that by lowering her voice God would not hear her or that by lowering her veil God would not see her laugh. But a half-laugh through clenched teeth could not fool God. God saw; God heard. "Yes, you did laugh," the angelic guest noted. Nothing is private with God, especially doubt. Sarah doubted God's unlimited power.

Learning from Sarah

We should be careful not to judge Sarah too critically, for we'd laugh too, if we were in her shoes. As a matter of fact, though we're not near ninety and have no chance or need for pregnancy, we laugh at other potential miracles that could happen to us or through us.

Poor health may be the reason some can't continue to serve. But usually it is not the hardening of arteries but the hardening of attitudes that keeps us on the sidelines. Rigidity of programming is one of the perils of seniorhood. We give up on others. We give up on ourselves. Do we not, like Sarah, think we know more than God? However, God is not done with us, though we are done with ourselves.

Some people and organizational structures actually sin against senior citizens. The opportunities for us to work in God's kingdom are withheld, denied, or discouraged by those who, like Sarah, think that God is done with those past their prime. Christians can be crippled by such apprehension so that useful spiritual Sarahs and Abrahams are never given ample opportunities in evangelism, in community aid programs, and in worship services.

What can we do?

Bev Shea is still singing beautifully though he is well into his eighties. What can *we* do to strengthen the local church, to energize God's prophets, to get the gospel out to an ink-dark society? God can use us in the far-reaching endeavors that we would naturally dismiss.

A volunteer senior force can make a church effective. Many are not too old to sew, to pray, to sing, to usher, to teach. Either we are too bashful to volunteer or too unwilling to try. Why not go out of life maximizing our influence for Christ, instead of sitting around waiting for an escort of heavenly angels?

We know Abraham was not cynical about God's covenant, for he went through with the painful stipulation of being circumcised. Abraham did not beg off circumcision at ninety-nine (Genesis 17:26). If Abraham didn't believe God was able to fulfill his end of the covenant, he wouldn't have gone through with this procedure. Circumcision is not for sissies. Circumcision at ninety-nine may have been as painful as having a baby at ninety. But Abraham was an enterprising senior, a daring centenarian. He didn't say, "Why bother?" It showed that Abraham was open to God, willing to hold up his end of the covenant sanction and submit to God's will.

As for Sarah, she needed elasticity in her beliefs more than flexibility in her body. She was still quite threatened by the presence of Hagar and her son, even after she laughed with God at Isaac's birth. Sarah had not lightened up toward Hagar. Tension increased rather than diminished. Hagar and Ishmael were finally forced from Abraham's dwelling. Though ninety, Sarah still had to grow up.

When looking at Sarah's doubt and cynicism, we might wonder why she was included among those of great faith, as named in Hebrews 11. Perhaps the proportions of her trust grew as more years passed. Or maybe her obedience to God during all those childless years was counted as faith—it certainly was faithfulness! More than likely, Sarah's faith went through highs and lows, just as ours does. We glimpse but a few scattered events in her life; we have no way of knowing the kind of faith Sarah demonstrated in areas of her life other than the painful one of childlessness.

More than likely Sarah came to understand the cosmic consequences of Isaac's arrival, that he would be the channel through whom multitudes would admire God (Genesis 21:6). Eventually she would learn that she could not keep Isaac to herself, that through him uncounted nations would be blessed. We can imagine that her vision went ahead to distant centuries when God would be sought by those outside Israel. A universal extension of God's kingdom would be channeled first through Isaac, then ultimately through the promised Redeemer.

Jesus is our Isaac

Israel's future rested in Isaac, and our future rests in Christ. When we put our faith in Christ, we can laugh with God at the inadequacy of by-passed substitute hopes. Enjoy the promise of God through Jesus Christ, for God's promise is as good as the deed done.

Worldly wisdom says, "We can't be sure of final salvation before its arrival. It is absurd and laughable to claim salvation when we are still sinners." But as Sarah discovered, as Abraham found, God's Word is the guarantee of its own fulfillment. The future is as sure as the past. That is the nature of Christian hope. As Isaac's promised coming could be counted on, despite the immense obstacles, so our final salvation is a sure thing. We can be as sure of being in heaven as we are sure Christ is in heaven. Preposterous? Presumptuous? No, for God can be counted on to keep his Word.

Isaac's arrival gave Sarah a new laugh, a laugh of absolute assurance. Similarly, with the arrival of Christ in our hearts, the joyful sound of the eternal ages is heard, felt, and enjoyed. We are *already* seated with Christ in heaven, though we are still on the earth (Ephesians 2:6). We are *already* citizens of the heavenly Jerusalem, although we still reside in an earthly structure (Philippians 3:20). We are said to be *already* glorified (aorist tense, Romans 8:30), although our actual glorification is ahead in our resurrection.

Laugh with God! Human feebleness, human spiritual infertility cannot stop Christ from being born in us. We have no reason to worry about losing the salvation ahead. Fixed on Christ, we have every reason to laugh.

When, his sons from bonds redeeming,
God to Zion led the way,
We were like to people dreaming
Thoughts of bliss too bright to stay.
Fill'd with laughter, stood we gazing,
Loud our tongues in rapture sang;
Quickly with the news amazing
All the startled nations sang.
"See Jehovah's works of glory!
Mark what love for them he had!"
"Yes, for us!" Go tell the story
This was done and we were glad.
—*Unknown*

Things to think about:

1. Do your reactions to delays resemble Sarah's in any way? What can prevent your laughter from turning cynical?

2. What effects do pain and disappointment have on faith? What insights from Sarah's story help you in puzzling, pounding trials?

3. Many serious-minded Christians dispute that faith and humor can coexist. When have you seen serious trust walk alongside hilarious laughter?

6

Moses: A Senior Homebody

Moses began his eightieth year
with God's promise at the burning bush—
"I will be with you" (Exodus 3:12).
Long afterwards, near the end of Israel's desert
wandering, Moses gladly acknowledged that God was
Israel's ultimate destination, their final home.
"O Lord, Thou hast been our home in successive
generations" (Psalm 90:1, New Berkley Version).
God as home was a priceless truth Moses reinforced
in his last public address (Deuteronomy 33:27).
His psalm-prayer, dated near the death
of his sister Miriam, began with a reminder
of where believing hearts loved to live.

J. GILMORE

ONE OF TODAY'S GREATEST TRAGEDIES IS THE UNSTABLE state of many homes. They have become battle zones, sad sites where ugly scenes shatter family closeness. Tempers erupt, arguments wound, animosities deepen, and distances lengthen. Once-tranquil homes have become places where children, wives, and husbands are abused instead of sheltered, humiliated instead of affirmed, and ridiculed instead of reassured.

Moses saw God as a place of refuge and comfort. God was like the ideal home. *The Good News Bible*'s translation of Moses' only psalm (Psalm 90) reads—"Lord, you have always been our home." Moses wandered a lot through sand and he pitched many tents, but for him there was only one home—God!

Another tragedy of our day is homelessness. What we once thought of as confined to crowded Bombay, India, where outcasts roam the streets, has become commonplace in affluent America. Cities of all sizes now have people who live in cardboard boxes, under plastic sheets and dirty blankets, or over subway grates. They call abandoned cars and condemned buildings "home." Whole families have been forced to sleep under bridges and on park benches. Stairwells of public garages and vents from office buildings are their bedrooms. It is a sad state.

The enormity of the homeless problem is hard to grasp. Local programs such as Cincinnati's "Tender Mercies" are seeking to remedy this problem. Similar efforts elsewhere are helping bring a touch of home to those who have no shelter.

Spiritual Homelessness

Foundational to these obvious societal problems is spiritual homelessness. Even in affluent houses, many have never made God their home. A cozy and classy house can never replace God.

Moses extolled God's adequacy to shelter and satisfy diverse humans. He also saw God in charge of history. Successive generations were dependent on God. Moses used three of God's names in Psalm 90:

1. Adoni (90:1), God as sovereign Lord
2. Yahweh (90:13), God a promise keeper

3. Yahweh Elohim (90:17), God the all powerful

Moses was praising and commending God when he said, "Lord, You have always been our home." Each generation has rediscovered the greatness, fullness, and adequacy of God. Belief in the Lord as sovereign, as promise keeper, and as powerful accomplisher was not just the whim of one generation. Throughout history individuals as well as entire nations have discovered that God is the place to be. He is not a halfway house to normalcy nor a weekend cabin in the mountains, but our best, our constant, and our truest home.

God does not expect Christian seniors to give up their homes and hit the road. That kind of expectation or deduction from Jesus' and Moses' lives is unwarranted and fallacious. Jesus did not berate his aging mother or his younger brothers for making Capernaum their home.

At some point, however, seniors must leave their dwellings, modest or magnificent. Relocation to an unfamiliar hospital room, or scaling down from a two-story house to a one-bedroom apartment can be traumatic. Living in a place where you no longer have unrestricted access to the kitchen can be a difficult adjustment. Some seniors find such transitions disturbing; parting with the familiar is painful. On the other hand, others see moving as a new challenge. A new location means making new friends. That, in itself, is challenging and can be very satisfying.

Moves can get our mental juices flowing so that we ponder, "Where is home? What is home?" The home where many Christians find the greatest tranquility is the house of God, the place where the Word of God is read, preached, and believed. Seniors, wherever they live, should find a sense of real security in their church homes, where they can always find other members of God's eternal family.

Some seniors make the mistake of not going to church. As the bones get creakier and our bodies' engines become harder to get started in the mornings, it becomes easier to sit in our houses on the Lord's Day. But being with God's people in assembly is exciting and fulfilling. When church is a second home, seniors discover an in-family refreshment. But going to church for an occasional visit, such as during Christmas or on Easter, is hardly getting to know God as a resting place and as a true home.

Moses was a homebody. One can be well-traveled and still consider home the favorite place to be. Moses had more mileage on him than any senior before or since, yet he liked to be home. His main dwelling—his constant home even when traveling—was God.

Whether we live in an apartment or whether we are homeowners, considering God as our best dwelling place lends power and poise to our lives. Moses knew the worth of a home. And he pointed his migrant comrades to God, their true home. The frustration, despair, and tiredness of desert transiency were reasons enough to look to God as a resting place as well as a place to get energized for the long days of wandering. When we find our secure place with the Lord, we become invigorated to face anything the world has to dish out. "The one who is in you is greater than the one who is in the world" (1 John 4:4). Not only is God's "home" for us found in church; he has placed it in our very selves as well.

Moses' Experience

For forty years of Moses' life he was a nomadic wanderer. Imagine, for forty years Moses had no home address. He was a sort of displaced person, a transient, a refugee. Being constantly on the move meant he was one of the homeless. If tax collectors mailed forms then, they wouldn't know where to send Moses'.

Moses once lived in a beautiful home. He had it very nice in his youth. Recall the privileges of the Egyptian royalty he enjoyed. Pharaoh's palace was Moses' boyhood home. Not bad. He was educated in all the wisdom of the Egyptians, and he was enriched with all the wealth of the Pharaoh. Moses' teen years were surrounded with opulence and abundance.

When Moses fled Egypt he kissed his cozy circumstances good-bye (Hebrews 11:24-27). Imagine the difficulty of leaving luxury and lavish living for a life of uncertainty, of privation, of foot-weary walking. Instead of strolling among the columned porches, he would have to dodge thorn bushes on mountain sides and trudge through tiring sand. He accepted a primitive life over a plentiful life in order to identify with his people. Home for him was no longer a permanent palace but a portable tent.

Did Moses really consider Pharaoh's palace home? Once he had met the Lord God, probably not. The gaudy life of an Egyptian prince could not fill the void in Moses for fellowship with God. Moses spoke out of the depth of his own experience when he said, "Lord, you have always been our home." He was speaking for himself, not just for his nation. God was the home his heart had searched for since his youth.

When you make God your home, whether as a teen or as a senior, it means that you stay and hear him out. You settle down with him and consider him your best friend. You talk with him about your problems, your projects, and your plans. You feel free to share your deepest longings, hurts, and goals. It means you allow him access to your hopes and dreams, thoughts and intentions. Moses did. Do we?

We lose our appreciation for the sheer pleasure of having a place we call "home." One commentator observed that it was "probably the houseless wandering of the Israelites in the wilderness which made them sensible to the value of habitation."[1]

Moses' Example

What if Moses could get into a time machine, push a button, and visit us? What would he say about our modern world, whether here or in Europe or elsewhere?

Would he find us living with the Lord? He would, doubtless, be appalled at those who cherish their privacy to the point of excluding God.

As Christians we have two dwellings: one where we live, eat, and sleep and one where we reside spiritually. "Lord, you have always been our home."

Home life with God takes time. We aren't really at home with God unless we spend evenings with him, unless we begin the day with him. Even though we make daily entrances into the whirl of worldly activities, we head home to God for rest and refreshment. The Christian goes home to God to unwind, to lay back, to receive nourishment from the banquet table of God's love and truth.

Moses led the Jews by example as well as by teaching. Because Moses demonstrated that God was important in his own life, that God was his true home, he left a lasting impression on his associates and his people. He was called "man of God" several times (Deuteronomy 33:1; Joshua 14:6; Psalm 90:1; 1 Chronicles 23:14; Ezra 3:2). Moses fellowshipped with God on Mt. Sinai (or Horeb), so that, in leading Israel, he was unaware that his face glowed. Moses had prostrated himself frequently at God's inner sanctum when he prayed for the nation of Israel.

Moses felt comfortable with God. Others may feel edgy around God. Jean Paul Sartre said that he learned to dislike God because his grandparents, who raised him, only "believed in God long enough to enjoy a toccata [a short organ piece]." Of his grandfather, Sartre wrote, "He hardly ever thought of God except in big moments." Then, in one of the saddest lines in his autobiography, he wrote, "I was led to disbelief not by the conflict of dogmas, but by my grandparents' indifference."[2]

For the lambs will follow the sheep you know,
Wherever the sheep may stray;
When the sheep go wrong, it will not be long
Till the lambs are as wrong as they.
—*Unknown*

Moses' Exhortation

Americans have been called modern nomads, for they move often—as many as four times in the average lifetime. To live in one location, in one house, is now the exception rather than the rule.

In one sense, it doesn't matter what our geographical address is. It doesn't matter whether we live in the North or the South, in the East or the West. When I left the West to move back East, a pastor asked me why I was leaving the West, "God's country." I said, "Wait a minute. For a Christian, *everywhere* is God's country!" Ironically, as God would have it, that pastor was later called to a church away from the beautiful Rocky Mountains.

The main thing is not where we serve God, but that we have God as our home. Augustine prayed, "You have made us for yourself and our hearts are restless until

they rest in you." Because we are made by God and for
God, we can be homesick even in our nicely kept houses.

> The British lawyer, William Blackstone, once defined a home
> as "that place from which when a man has departed, he is a
> wanderer until he has returned."

Man once began with God. He was dwelling with
God, but through sin, he left home. Adam wanted to
avoid God, hide from God, and flee from God. So sin
alienates us from God. We want to build our lives on
self-satisfying values, rather than on glorifying God. Sin
makes us think of God as a big bore. We prefer to get as
far away from him as possible, rather than seeking his
company.

Blackstone's definition of home is even more true of
people spiritually than spatially. "We are wanderers until
we return." Returning to God as home is more than coming back to church. Of course, that can be a start. But we
must learn to feel so much at home with God that we go
to him every day, not just on Sunday. God should not be
our last resort, but as the psalmist says (71:3, KJV), our
continual resort.

Feeling free is the feeling of home. There we can dress
the way we want and not feel we've done wrong. We can
spill milk and not become embarrassed. We can be ourselves without being rejected. We don't have to look like
we've stepped out of a show case or come from a beauty
parlor. Home means we can mess up and make mistakes,
yet still be loved. We may be playfully put down, but not
forcefully pushed out. That's home.

Moses prodded his people as he prayed with them.
"Lord, You have always been our home." We, too, dis-

cover God as our home when we can unburden ourselves before him.

Too many times prayers are not conversations with God, but the dropping off of a want list at his front door. Then we speed off to someone else. Or we knock but are unwilling to meet God when he opens the door.

> What a friend we have in Jesus,
> All our sins and griefs to bear,
> What a privilege to carry,
> Everything to God in prayer.
> —*Joseph Scriven*

Notice in Psalm 90 that Moses didn't drop off his requests and then hurry off. For the first eleven verses of the psalm Moses was occupied with God's *person*. It was only in verses 12-17 that he engaged in petitioning God and in making requests. That's what it means to settle down with God, to make God our spiritual home.

In other words, we make God our home when we unpack our private feelings. We make him our reference point. His standards become the criteria of the way we live instead of our using the world's standards to judge God. Making God our home means we are willing to spend time with him, to "let our hair down" and allow him to speak with us.

In the 70s we lived in Worland, Wyoming. Then it had a population of about six thousand. The now-defunct Frontier Airline had four flights into Worland's airport each day. And there were many privately owned airplanes there. Some of the locals would use their planes to spot herds of elk in the mountains for the eastern hunters who would spend big bucks to bag an elk.

Those who took up flying practiced the technique of "touch and go." This was accomplished by making a landing, then continuing the flight by immediately taking off again.

When it comes to prayer, there are times when we must say a short prayer and then engage in other duties. But there are also times in prayer when we should fully land. It is hardly home if the only conversation is to stick our heads inside the door and say something on our way. It would make a person feel that he or she was being used, not enjoyed.

What a shame that we give God cause to feel this way—used, when his welcome mat is always out, the light is always in the window, and the door is unlocked no matter how late the hour. He will never turn us out when we return. He is always in, ready to hear us out, once we enter. Like the father in the parable of the prodigal son, he is willing to welcome us with a feast. God does not treat us the way many treat him.

It's just a good thing God above
Has never closed His door,
Because He wasn't treated fair,
Or called one great big bore.
If He had ever once sat down
And said, "That's it—I'm through:
I've had enough of those on earth,
So this is what I'll do.
I'll give my orders to the sun,
Cut off your heat supply,
And to the moon—'Give no more light.'
And 'Run those oceans dry.'
Then (just to make it really tough
And put the pressure on),

Turn off the air and oxygen."
We know He'd be quite justified,
If fairness was the game,
For no one has been more abused
Or treated with disdain,
Yet He carries on, supplying you and me,
With all the favors of His grace,
And everything for free.
Kids say they want a better deal
And so they split and go,
But what a deal we've given God,
To whom all goods we owe.
We don't care who we hurt or harm,
To gain some things and more,
But what a mess we'd all be in
If God should slam the door.
—*Unknown*

When you want a sturdy house built, you get the best architect and the most experienced carpenters to do the job. Perpetual tent-living can't compare to living in a house. Houses are meant to be permanent shelters: dry, heated, cool, and clean.

Another Example: Jesus

The Lord Jesus had the benefit of being raised in a godly, but modest home. Like his foster father, Joseph, he developed a carpenter's keen eye. He knew a poorly constructed house when he saw one. In fact, he used a badly built house as an illustration of a person whose life script collapses when not solidly built on God's teachings.

Though Jesus could have built himself a home, he did not. He later told his disciples that he was going ahead to heaven to design and construct rooms for them! Our Lord chose the life of an itinerant evangelist. "Foxes have holes, and birds of the air have nests; but the Son of man has nowhere to lay his head" (Matthew 8:20, RSV). A life of ministry requires the possibility of frequent moves. The luxury of a settled home life is not guaranteed when one decides to preach the gospel full-time.

Our Lord left his home above to visit us on earth. His ascension into heaven was his return home. His greatest desire was to have us live with him forever in the glorious heavenly city.

We long for an eternal home. God wants us to live with him on earth so that living with him eternally is not a new experience. Do not pass up daily contact with God; don't just visit him. Live with him, year in and year out, and for all eternity.

Things to think about:

1. Out of the different houses you have lived in during your life, which ones did you feel most comfortable in? Why?

2. How is God like a home to you?

3. How do you think heaven will be like home?

(See John Gilmore, *Probing Heaven,* [Baker Book House, 1989, 1991-3rd printing], pp. 83, 175-176, 270, 280-281.)

7

Caleb: A Senior Dynamo

[Caleb] is one of the sunniest characters
of the Bible. His whole story might have been written
with a pen dipped in sunshine. . . . Was there ever
a cheerier man of eighty-five years? His cheerfulness
sprang from his godliness. It was a stream from a fount
in the eternal heights. He had wholly followed the Lord
and gladness had been his portion. When evening
shadows rested on his head eternal sunshine
settled in his heart.
DINSDALE T. YOUNG

So-CALLED "OLD PEOPLE" ARE SURPRISINGLY PHYSICALLY
durable. Consider that ice hockey wizard, Gordie Howe,
the "grandfather" of the National Hockey League. He set
NHL records for most games, most goals, most assists,
and most points! He came out of retirement to play
again.

Aging poses even less limitations on artistic talent.
Grandma Moses began to paint landscapes at age seventy-
eight! Creative juices flow in the elderly, too.

Caleb was gifted both with enduring physical strength
and mental agility. At age eighty-five Caleb wasn't content to sit whittling wood on his front porch. He may
have had a fiery youth, but he wasn't a mere smoldering

ember at eighty-five. No, Caleb was one of Israel's best-known sparks. Now, epochs after his demise, we are still drawn to the brightness of his flame.

Caleb was an Old Testament model oldster, a hero in its Senior Hall of Fame. At age eighty-five, when other men had given up, Caleb retained most of what he had been at forty. In his own words from Joshua 14:11: "I am still as strong today as the day Moses sent me out; I'm just as vigorous to go out to battle now as I was then." He was not puffed up with bravado, but he was brave. His outlook was still bright; his mind was still sharp.

Caleb earned a name as leader of his district (Joshua 14:14). He was a favorite son of his region, an honorary prince of Judah. Later, he was considered chief of the Hezronites in southern Canaan.

Caleb was exciting and enterprising. His character shone through two key events. Attractively upbeat, engaging, and spiritual, he is an inspiration to seniors at any age, in any decade.

Caleb at Forty Years of Age

Two years after the Exodus from Egypt, Israel was camped at Kadesh Barnea. Caleb was chosen to be one of twelve spies (one from each tribal area) to enter Hebron and the surrounding district to report back on its fertility, fortifications, and occupants. Moses' order was that a para-military incursion of limited size and duration was needed to check out what was ahead so that Israel would not be taken by surprise.

Caleb's first appearance in Scripture was at the mass rally where the returning spies gave their report. The meeting was the occasion for a famous "Good News/Bad News" speech.[1]

The majority report was mostly negative, even though the gigantic grape samples they brought back on bows were a good sign of the land's agricultural richness.

The minority report by Joshua and Caleb encouraged immediate attack and advance. Caleb must have had a powerful, penetrating voice, for he was able to quiet the large assembly.

> Then [after the bad report] Caleb silenced the people before Moses and said, "We should go up and take possession of the land, for we can certainly do it." *Numbers 13:30*

The other ten spies, however, had a chance to rebut Caleb's recommendation. The majority report ended with a gloomy statement:

> And they spread among the Israelites a bad report about the land they had explored. They said, "The land we explored devours those living in it. All the people we saw there are of great size. We saw the Nephilim there (the descendants of Anak come from the Nephilim). We seemed like grasshoppers in our own eyes and we looked the same to them." *Numbers 13:32-33*

Following that a chorus of grumbling began to work through the crowd. And it was Moses and Aaron who felt the heat (Numbers 14:1-4).

The people were preoccupied with defeat. They foresaw calamity and annihilation. They quickly forgot all that the Lord had brought them through. A "dump Moses" campaign began (Numbers 14:36-37) on the heels of the bad majority report. And, because of Israel's unbelief that immobilized them and stopped them from taking Canaan, they were to wander forty years in the desert (one year for each of the forty days it took the reconnaissance band to complete their exploration).

Two moral qualities came forward in the life of Caleb on this occasion.

Caleb's optimism

Twix optimist and pessimist
The difference is droll;
The optimist sees the doughnut,
The pessimist sees the hole.
—*Unknown*

Caleb was not swayed by this great wind of pessimism. He was the kind of fisherman who would pack some tartar sauce in his tackle box. He would agree with the great lexicographer, Samuel Johnson, who said, "Nothing will ever be attempted if all possible objections must be first overcome." He would agree even more with the Lord Jesus, who said, "Everything is possible for him who believes" (Mark 9:23).

Caleb's courage

Caleb's backbone was immune to the yellow streak. He believed in the ability of God to bring victory through the efforts of his people. He trusted that their deficiencies would be covered by God's goodness and blessed with his power.

The weight of ten other opinions didn't topple Caleb; he was not a domino, but a dynamo. Moses heard Caleb contradict the dismal outlook of the ten spies and he greatly admired him, as did God. (Caleb's tenacity *against* the ten spies reminded Moses of his own earlier tenacity *for* the Ten Commandments.)

Recall that Moses had not taken polls along the way to see whether or not Israel wanted to go where God led or to accept his Ten Commandments. Likewise, Caleb did not go either by the pessimism of the spies or by the pleas of the people. He took to heart the statement of Moses earlier, in Exodus 23:2—"You must not follow a majority to do wrong" (Moffatt translation).[2]

Caleb was bold, resolute, and courageous to buck the "Dump Moses" and "Back to Egypt" spirit of the people. God saw the raw courage of Caleb, and of it he said to Moses:

> **B**ecause my servant Caleb was of a different spirit and follows me wholeheartedly, I will bring him into the land he went to, and his descendants will inherit it. *Numbers 14:24*

Caleb did not buckle under disdain, nor abandon his position when derided. The people's contempt for him was as real as the complaints they had for Moses and Aaron. How contemptuous were the people? Enough to threaten to stone them (Numbers 14:10).

The angry crowd came to the point of hurling rocks and crushing skulls. Moses and Aaron were astonished, ashamed, and aghast. They dropped to the ground in prayer as if their feet had been knocked out from under them (14:5). Joshua and Caleb tore their clothes indicating that the people were blaspheming God by their unbelieving attitude (14:6).

Then Caleb gave his second speech, recorded in Numbers 14:7-9. He took the high ground, reaffirming the great value of the land ahead, its present productivity and its continued fertility. Then he repeated his conviction that the Hebron district could be taken with the

Lord's help. "If the Lord is pleased. . . . Their protection is gone, but the Lord is with us" (Numbers 14:8-9). Caleb's speech called them to view the Lord's earlier promise not just as a pie-in-the-sky dream. He reminded them of the solemnity of refusing God's directions, and, finally, urged them to put aside their fears (twice saying, "Do not be afraid!").

The dissenting mob Caleb addressed was surly, negative, and vindictive. Their response? Cooperation? No. At this point they threatened to pelt Caleb and Joshua with rocks and pound them into silence. But God stepped in, acting as a shield. The Shekinah glory of God appeared (14:10) in the tabernacle. There God spoke to Moses at length. The babbling multitude had said enough.

Surely Moses, Caleb, and Joshua were enormously encouraged by the Lord's support. Through the following forty years of desert wandering Caleb would be sustained by God, by his wonderful words, and the prospect of seeing them fulfilled. For that loyalty God announced a land grant to Caleb, called "My servant," as a form of compensation for his distress in the line of duty (14:24).

Caleb at Eighty-Five

Caleb's third speech appears in Joshua 14, given when he was eighty-five. The speech was partly a review (showing an exact memory) and partly an exhortation to Joshua (showing a determined man). This third speech was to Joshua personally, not to the Jewish people. The same fairness and forcefulness that marked his earlier talks are found in this one.

The speech gives the spirit of Caleb. He was not sappy and senile. As card players would say, he still had a full deck after forty years in the desert.

Caleb was an octogenarian with pizzazz. Let's look at what made him so strong at eighty-five.

Persistence
Caleb did not intend to speak to Joshua with small talk. What he had to say was prepared ahead of time. We can be fairly sure of this because he came to the occasion with a delegation from his district.

> Now the men of Judah approached Joshua at Gil-gal, and Caleb son of Jephunneh the Kenizzite said to him, "You know what the Lord said to Moses the man of God at Kadesh Barnea about you and me."
> *Joshua 14:6*

The Gilgal convocation had been called to draw lots and settle land claims in view of the fact that Israel's occupation of Canaan was almost complete. Everyone wanted a piece of the pie. The purpose of the national meeting was to decide what tribe got what land (Joshua 14:1-5).

Caleb had come to Joshua, not with a cheering section of relatives, but with the constitutional leaders of his province. The men were official representatives of the people and when Caleb spoke they knew, at least in essence, what he was going to say. What he had to say to Joshua was tribal in scope. It was not the petition of a greedy individual trying to cash in on some uncontested real estate.

Does a man in his eighties need land? If he got along as a nomad for forty-odd years, what are a few more years of being homeless! Caleb intended to receive the land due him, for God had specifically promised to Moses that Caleb would get the land of Hebron and its surrounding districts.

Caleb's persistence showed level-headed prudence. He gave an honest assessment of his productivity at eighty-five and clearly recognized the authority of the Word of God. When God took the trouble to tell Moses that Caleb would receive a specific territory, he meant it. And Caleb took God's promise seriously. Caleb persisted in believing that God's promise was valid despite the lapse of time.

Intentional
At his age Caleb could have thought his life was over and done with. But he didn't throw in the towel. He announced to Joshua that he was trim and kept training to do battle in the giant garrison of the Anakites.

> So here I am today, eighty-five years old. I am still as strong today as the day Moses sent me out. I'm just as vigorous to go out to battle now as I was then. *Joshua 24:10-11*

Caleb's determination reminds me of George Blanda. At forty-eight, he was considered a washout for professional football after having scored a record 2,002 points in 26 seasons. In 1976, after being waived by the Oakland Raiders, Blanda said, "I'm not crying because I know this is the end. I'm too old. If a team took me, they'd be nuts. But if they did, I'd go."[3]

Seniors give up too easily when it comes to keeping in shape. Sports writers have on file the many stories of men and women in their sixties, seventies, and eighties who have rediscovered the satisfaction of physical exercise. Just because we're past retirement doesn't mean we should pull up our oars and drift into obscurity. We may not set records, but we can keep ourselves from falling apart. With medical approval and sound nutrition, moderate to vigorous exercise has short- and long-term benefits.

Caleb was not the kind of man who thought or talked about retiring. He aimed to keep on contributing to life. He wanted to finish strong in the human race.

Two men shared a seat in a train. One was eighty-five. The other man said, "I envy your vigor. What is the secret of your astonishing vitality?" Laughing, the older gentleman said, "I'm living on the interest of a well-invested youth."

God told Moses that "Caleb has a different spirit" (Numbers 14:24). Indeed, fresh breezes blew off Caleb. It was that "different spirit" that kept Caleb young to the last days of his life.

Caleb was the kind of man who would like to swap stories with Sir Edmund Hillary, the first man to scale Mount Everest. When Sir Hillary turned sixty-one, he knew his days of high adventure on top of the world's highest peaks were numbered, but he wasn't ready to pass up every challenge. He said, "I don't like the thought of growing old gracefully, sitting under a palm."[4]

Industriousness was the result of Caleb's intentional lifestyle. He had goals. He didn't loll along. Instead of reacting, he acted. He didn't watch life, he participated. The Anakites felt the imprint of his energy and lived to regret that Israel had the likes of Caleb.

A hearty "hurrah!" to the seniors who keep their wits and get involved. Christian seniors should be engaged in enhancing the cause of Christ. When Archibald Alexander, the first professor at Princeton Theological Seminary, lay on his death bed, he exhorted those present, "As an aged man I would say to my fellow-pilgrims, 'endeavor to be useful as long as you are continued on earth.' "[5]

What then? Shall we sit idly down and say
The night hath come; it is no longer day?
The night hath not yet come; we are not quite
Cut off from labor by the failing light;
Something remains for us to do or dare;
Even the oldest trees some fruit may bear. . . .
For age is opportunity no less
Than youth itself, though in another dress,
And as the evening twilight fades away
The sky is filled with stars, invisible by day.
—*Henry Wadsworth Longfellow*

Cheerfulness

Seniors can become bitter. At age twenty, we worry about what others think of us. At fifty, we don't care what others think of us. At seventy we discover that people haven't been thinking of us. At eighty, we learn that people are glad to forget us.

Suspicion that others wish to intentionally snub us, slight us, or swindle us can sour our minds. Agatha Christie, the famous mystery novelist, wrote whimsically:

The sense of being a displaced person . . . makes so many elderly people indulge in the illusion that they are being poisoned or their belongings stolen. I don't think really it is a weakening of the mental faculties— it is an excitement that they need, a kind of stimulant: life would be more interesting if someone were trying to poison you.[6]

But suspicions can get ugly. Paranoid fears can petrify seniors. Is it this kind of paranoia that causes people to associate age with grouchiness and other negative personality flaws? Several years ago when we approached

Junction City, Kansas, there was a large billboard that read: "Welcome to Junction City, Kansas. Population: 20,236 Friendly People and 6 Old Grouches."

Shakespeare called it "crabbed age." Let's rather mimic Caleb for his exuberant cheerfulness. We can't imagine him looking over his shoulder to find what people were thinking of him. Rather, gratitude for a full and happy life bubbled up from the depths of his heart.

> "The Lord sent me from Kadesh Barnea to explore the land . . . [the Lord] has kept me alive for forty-five years since the time he said this to Moses. . . . the Lord helping me I will drive [the Anakites] out just as He said. . . ." *Joshua 14:7, 10, 12*

Caleb saw God in every circumstance. He saw God where others saw nothing but luck. We should smile, like Caleb, for no one is too small in God's love. No problems are too big for God's power. Rejoice in the Lord, for he will abundantly bless.

Several years ago an ad was carried in a major U.S. daily newspaper:

"Wanted: Lady's Companion
Must be a Christian
Cheerful if possible"

People are attracted to those whose cheerfulness is authentic, such as evangelist George Whitefield, a genuinely happy man. After the death of this eloquent evangelist a prominent New York woman was asked how Whitefield influenced her to trust Christ. She said, "Mr. Whitefield was so cheerful that it tempted me to become a Christian."[7]

Wholehearted in following God

The expression "wholehearted" used to describe Caleb has the nautical connotation of a sail hoisted to catch the wind. Caleb hadn't trimmed his sails, he hoisted and unfurled them to catch all the wind God would send him.

We can't have Caleb's joy without sharing his Lord. We cannot expect to know the heart harmony from which joy springs unless we live fully for God. We must believe wholeheartedly like Caleb.

> [God said to Moses] "Caleb has a different spirit and follows me wholeheartedly." *Numbers 14:24; Deuteronomy 1:36*
>
> [Caleb said] "I . . . followed the Lord my God wholeheartedly." *Joshua 14:8*

Caleb kept spiritually rejuvenated by God's goodness and mercy and God's consistency and unchangeableness in his promise. The promises of God had sustained Caleb with a happy fulfillment. And what helped Caleb can help us. God's dependability should be a source of great joy to us. We can rely on him to keep his promise.

Old man Johann Wolfgang von Goethe was able to finish Faust, his masterpiece, after sixty years of labor on it. He was a feisty old man at seventy-three when he boasted, "Under these white locks there is an Aetna (volcano)!" His many successful publications included a 12,111-line epic poem, five major dramas, four long novels, a ten-volume autobiography, and a six-volume work on color. Yet he lived with a storm cloud over his head. No wonder; he spoke of Christ as a fable and he didn't believe in a biblical heaven. Goethe said that one of his ambitions was to abolish the devil and plug up hell. But in the last hours of his life, he said:

"My life has been a tissue of pains and chagrins and out of my seventy-five years [as an adult] I cannot count four weeks of pure enjoyment."

Emil Ludwig commented on Goethe:

To his ninth decade Goethe remained what he had been in his third—religious but not a Christian, upright but not a moralist . . . a believer in Eternity but not in Judgment. The Christian teaching was to the end entirely alien to him, though the vehemence of his earlier attacks upon it had now been softened into irony. . . . The conclusion of Faust led to the fallacy that Goethe turned religious in old age. In reality Faust, like Goethe himself, shows no sign of a conscience or a longing for pardon.[8]

Caleb's spiritual dedication and his reliance on God's promise made him the exact opposite of Goethe. Caleb's secret to his constructive and cheerful life was following God fully and believing God's promises unreservedly and wholly.

Unless God is in constant control of the world, there is no reason to hope, no reason to pray, no reason to be happy. History and our lives are in God's hands and subject to his will. We have good reason to be joyful because God is alive, almighty, and active.

Things to think about

1. Name four things that make you happy. How is God in those things?

2. Do you think of optimists as naive or unintelligent? Do you think pessimists are usually realists?

3. What are two of your short-range goals? Long-range goals? Have you committed these goals to God, or are they merely wishes? What steps do you need to take in order to see your goals fulfilled?

8

Naomi: A Senior Who Trusted God in Tough Times

[Bethlehem's inhabitants] . . . all observed [Naomi]
closely as she entered the gates. Who could that
poor old woman be? Every feature of her face
betrayed lines of care and bereavement. . . .
[Naomi] thought clearly and logically and when she
spoke it was with eloquence and preciseness. . . . Her
concern was never with herself but always
with the child to whom the Lord had attached her [Ruth].
Thus Naomi subdued bitterness, and her former
pleasantness, entirely purged now, returned to her.
ABRAHAM KUYPER

SCRIPTURE SHOWS SENIORS IN TOUGH SPOTS AND FACING
rough circumstances for our benefit. How did biblical
seniors react when hit hard and how did they manage
when faced with harried choices? Biblical women, who
lived without Social Security and husbands' pension
funds, were especially vulnerable.

Naomi was a senior with whom many should easily
relate, for she knew the anguish and humiliation of being
without necessities. In the death of her husband and two
sons, Naomi suffered devastating personal loss. Hus-

bandless, she was confronted with long-lasting economic plight and loss of emotional support.

When she started out in life she never could have anticipated what was to follow. She married a Bethlehemite man, Elimelech. And God blessed them with two sons: Mahlon and Chilion. Soon afterwards, however, there was a severe famine in the region. Across the Jordan River, in the traditionally hostile border-country of Moab, Elimelech learned that there was food enough for his young family. He decided to bury Jewish dread and dislike for Moabites and move his family to where they could survive.

New troubles, however, met them in the land of Moab. Everything went well for a time, but then tragedy struck. Elimelech died, leaving Naomi with two sons to raise in a foreign culture. She stayed on and the boys married Moabite women. Mahlon married the Moabite girl Ruth, and Chilion married a young Moabitess named Orpah. But soon after their marriages, Naomi's sons died. Naomi met wall-to-wall widowhood. The women banded together in their grief.

While Ruth, the Moabitess (widow of one of Naomi's sons), is the central figure in the book of Ruth, her mother-in-law, Naomi, plays a decisive role. Naomi is often overlooked, yet she was a key character in the unfolding drama. Without Naomi the story of Ruth could not have happened. Her story is one of God's providence. God never took his hand off Naomi. By looking over her shoulder we learn how one senior woman handled hardship and how God used her to advance his plans.

Along with the actions of Ruth and Boaz, [Naomi's] shrewdness is the link which connects Yahweh's earlier direct intervention, the gift of food (1:6), with its sequel, the gift of conception (4:13).[1]

God's Plans Not Limited by Disaster

Elimelech and Naomi started life together as a husband and wife in the little town of Bethlehem. Bethlehem means "house of bread." Yet when famine struck, pantry shelves, grain barrels, and storage sheds soon emptied.

Moab was a high (two to three thousand feet) fertile plateau south of Bethlehem and visible from its hills. Unlike Bethlehem, Moab had not been hit with a failed harvest and famine, and it was readily accessible, about fifty miles away. Elimelech decided to take his wife and two boys into Moab, a move that many Israelites would have hesitated to make. Although the Moabites were loosely related to the Israelites, their national religion was much closer to that of the Canaanites. The circumstances of Elimelech's family must have been serious; they were acting in the interest of survival.

But Naomi ran against a worst-case scenario. Not only did her husband die, but within the space of about ten years, her two sons died also.

One of the themes of Naomi's life was how God worked in unexpected ways. God had reversed Bethlehem's fortune; the fertile fields yielded fresh food. Naomi was faced with the choice of staying put or venturing a return trip to Bethlehem.

The little town of Bethlehem was beginning to see its grocery bins bulge. Naomi's and Ruth's seeming coincidental arrival at the beginning of the harvest was not due to a stroke of luck, but due to the strategy of God. Without the barley harvest Ruth and Boaz would not have met and married. And Ruth's presence on Boaz's field was not a fluke. God was behind the so-called chance meeting, from which eventually came the heir through whose line Christ was born.

Left unstated, but clearly deductible from the facts of the story, was that God was immediately and immanently involved. And while God removed Naomi's husband and her two sons, he also gave her two loving daughters-in-law. He gave Ruth the desire to stay with Naomi. God also provided Ruth and Naomi a kinsman redeemer. The bringing together of Ruth and Boaz and the eventual birth of Obed were all parts of God's intervention and action. But that did not deny the human element or diminish the importance of Naomi's role in advising Ruth how to get Boaz's attention and affection. "His unseen presence causes human actions to succeed."[2]

We can learn from Naomi to go from tragedy to triumph. New futures break through dead-ends and defeat. "Weeping may remain for a night, but rejoicing comes in the morning" (Psalm 30:5).

Whenever we are afflicted, God is not hounding us for lack of devotion so much as *he is reminding us that new opportunities result from his grace.* New horizons appear in God's will where once we saw blocked progress and bleak prospects.

If our dear Lord did not put these thorns under our head, we should sleep out our lives, and lose our glory.—*Richard Baxter*

A Special Mother-Daughter Relationship

When Naomi, Ruth, and Orpah got to the border between Moab and Israel, Naomi expected to continue alone and to let her two young daughters-in-law go back to Moab and begin a new life by remarrying. Orpah exercised the option of returning to her roots. Although she loved Naomi, she decided that returning home was what she wanted. Ruth, however, did not want to leave Naomi and was willing to risk an unknown future in a land where Moabites were looked on with scorn. The farewell scene, early on in the book of Ruth, is one of the more famous good-byes in the Bible. Alongside the farewell between David and Barzillai, and Paul and the Ephesian elders, it is one of the most touching scenes in Scripture.

One amazing feature of the farewell was that the two daughters-in-law showed genuine love for their mother-in-law. There was nothing stilted, formal, or phony about their mutual displays of affection. Sorrow and sharing had welded them together in a bond of true love.

Mothers-in-law are routinely chided for grudge-holding and meddlesomeness. Naomi, however, was neither bossy nor moody. She was an ideal mother-in-law—noncontemptuous, nonmanipulative, and nonintrusive. She did not insist on having her own way.

At the time of the border-crossing, Naomi laid out the options objectively and realistically.

- Naomi was not going to have any more sons.
- Even if she had sons immediately, the young women were not going to wait until they grew.
- And it would be unreasonable to turn down suitors in order to comply with Old Testament custom.

Naomi's insistence could have indicated that she was overbearing, seeking to plan their lives for them. Rather, Naomi wanted them to know she wished their decision to be unfettered by false guilt. She didn't make them feel that they loved her less if they decided to return to Moab. In that way Naomi showed that she was nonpreferential and allowed their decisions to be wholly their own.

Naomi stated in straightforward terms that for the young women to go with her inevitably meant that they would be abandoning hope for remarriage.[3] Though Naomi seemed to discourage the girls with that comment, it was really her way of showing neutrality, a willingness to abide by their decision.

Ruth's response was one of the great affirmations of the meaning of love:

> Don't urge me to leave you or to turn back from you. Where you go I will go, and where you stay I will stay. Your people will be my people and your God my God. *Ruth 1:16*

Ruth showed that her decision was influenced by her keen interest in being a follower of Yahweh. She was drawn to Naomi's God, not just to the companionship of Naomi.

How did Ruth come to that commitment? What drew her to Yahweh? Ruth wanted to forsake her Moabite god, Chemosh, and follow the Lord. Why?

Ruth's wonderful statement of intent did not arise out of a total vacuum but was the result of long months of association. Undoubtedly, Naomi talked about her God and shared her faith. Ruth's attraction to the Lord was the result of Naomi's witness to God's goodness. Naomi had probably spoken of God's deliverance of Israel from Egypt at the Exodus—the central story of Israel's history and one repeated often within families and communities. She may have also referred to the crossing-over in faith of another non-Jewess, Rahab, during Joshua's time. Naomi's faith was the impetus for Ruth's faith.

Naomi had previously modeled the style of faith that Ruth expressed:

> Behind all the nobleness, steadfastness, beauty, and tenderness of Ruth, I see inspiring, sustaining, and maturing it all, the wise, chastened, weaned mind of one who was a mother in Israel (Naomi).[4]

Yet it seems we must go another step in trying to discover how Ruth could make the drastic move from Moabite worship to monotheistic faith. Ultimately, it was not just the example of Naomi, but the expression of the power of God himself. The Spirit of God gave Ruth strength to turn her back on her past—realizing that her family would disown her—and risk her future with a nation traditionally mistreated and maligned by Moabites. I agree with George Lawson:

> Unless she had been drawn by that divine power, which alone can change the hearts of men, she would not have come to the Lord's land, and to God himself as her exceeding joy.[5]

The personal bond between Naomi and Ruth that had grown over several significant years was used by the Holy Spirit to move Ruth toward this risk of faith.

Do you ever think your faith has counted for nothing? Ever wonder what good you do by letting down your spiritual hair with friends and relatives? Ever despair that your prayers have gone unheard? Naomi's impact on Ruth should remind us that God can use our example of faith in the Lord to lead relatives, whose backgrounds have been pagan, whose earliest impressions of believers have been negative, to influence them toward the Christian faith.

Naomi's Return to Bethlehem

When Naomi re-entered Bethlehem after ten years' absence and turbulent personal tragedies, her physical appearance showed significant change. It was not just Bethlehemite women's poor memories that made them unsure it was Naomi. She looked old. Townsfolk asked,

"Can this be Naomi?" What ten years of stress can do to woman or man! Naomi had been through more than they realized. Cosmetics could not cover, hide, or erase Naomi's dark lines and deepening wrinkles.

Naomi understood their surprise. Her response was to play out the significance of her name, which meant "delight" or "happy." She said, "Don't call me 'Naomi,' but call me 'Mara.'" Mara meant "bitter." "Call me 'Bitter,' because . . . the Almighty has made my life very bitter" (1:20).

Naomi acknowledged the detrimental effect her sorrow had had on her looks, without taking offense at the women's astonishment. She had left town with three males and returned with none. She left with plenty but returned empty. Openly she confessed, "The Almighty has brought misfortune upon me" (1:21).

How are we to take her comments? Were they bitter reflections, or were they a balanced acceptance of the effects her troubles had on her appearance? Was her attribution of her troubles to God a complaint, or did she speak matter-of-factly, an indication that bitterness had not taken root in her heart?

On the surface it might seem that Naomi felt mistreated by God. Naomi's prior reaction to the deaths of her husband and sons showed that bitterness had not entirely settled out of her life. Her remarks to the Bethlehem citizens indicated that. She admitted that God had made her taste some bitter experiences.

We unfairly stretch her comments if we say she seethed with resentment or boiled with rage. Rather she recognized that God had chosen trials for her: "The Almighty has brought misfortune upon me." She did not deny that God, in his sovereignty, had caused her to experience disappointment and loss.

Her experience of standing at three freshly dug graves was unimaginably difficult. She had not minimized her troubles, but she now saw God in them and God behind them. God used her darkest moments to bring her to her senses—to increase, deepen, and sharpen her sense of God's lordship. Life had been bitter, but she was not bitter. In her sorrows, God had done something wonderful, something lasting, something beneficial. She saw her pain through God's lens. Like Job, her experiences had enabled her to see God more clearly—as who he was, rather than who she may have supposed him to be.

[Naomi had] the bitterness of grief, not of impatience. She is very deeply humbled under the mighty hand of God, but does not fret at the dispensations of his providence.[6]

The late Swiss psychiatrist, Paul Tournier, pointed out that an adult woman could carry throughout her life an unresolved conflict from her youth and perpetuate it, relive it, and revive it, to her detriment, time after time. He shared the case of

. . . an elderly lady, because as a child she never could accept the death of her father except as an injustice to her, has all her life had an attitude of having been wronged . . . [which undoubtedly had ruined her ability to have a deep and lasting relationship with other men] . . . Bitterness related to lost loved ones is especially painful and difficult, for nothing can eradicate it except a spiritual miracle.[7]

The women of Bethlehem detected peace of mind in Naomi. They pronounced the following beautiful benediction:

Praise be to the LORD, who this day has not left you without a kinsman-redeemer. May he become famous throughout Israel! He will renew your life and sustain you in your old age. *For your daughter-in-law, who loves you and who is better to you than seven sons, has given him birth. Ruth 4:14-15*

Five wonderful traits stand out in this senior woman:

Naomi exercised objectivity in surveying her options

Naomi outlined her prospects, good and bad, before she made up her mind about which one to pursue. Seniors today need to be equally level-headed. The consequences of choices, long-term versus short-term, weigh upon us for decision, whether it has to do with where to live or what surgery to elect or not elect, and other equally important decisions. Just because we are Christians does not mean we can escape hard choices. The choices we face will probably not be between what is pleasurable and what is painful, but which of the painful options we are best able to handle!

Naomi lived close to God

Ruth saw Naomi suffer in her triple losses. She was impressed by the way she grieved and how she recovered. It must have been something like the resiliency that Frances Havergal expressed in her lines:

> Every joy or trial falleth from above,
> Traced upon our dial, by the Son of love.
> We may trust Him fully, all for us to do,
> They who trust Him wholly, find Him wholly true.

Naomi's grit and godliness

Naomi was instrumental in getting Ruth married to Boaz. She coached Ruth on how to get his attention and admiration. Naomi gave Ruth advice in noble coquetry and the custom of coming under the legal umbrella of a kinsman-redeemer. We don't have space to deal with the steps in the courting process, except to note that Naomi played a significant role as matchmaker. By having encouraged Ruth to dress and smell like a bride, she helped Boaz to think of Ruth as a bride. This was an interesting case of the woman taking initiative in the courting process!

Naomi was genuinely unselfish

Naomi escaped the tendency of some mothers-in-law—of wanting to dictate to their daughter(s)-in-law. A mother who cannot give up her children, when of age, to act responsibly and to chart their own courses shows that she is unable to surrender them to the Lord. Too many young couples have found adjustment in marriage difficult because of an interfering mother-in-law. Naomi didn't shy away from giving positive advice once Ruth had picked her own objective. Yet Naomi, who had not tried to manipulate Ruth into following her into Bethlehem, would not turn upon Ruth as a ruthless orchestrator of her future. She was content to see the romance deepen, blossom, and produce lasting fruit.

Naomi exalted God even over her own welfare

Both the famine and the funerals were untimely, agonizing, and wrenching. But Naomi must have turned to God during those trials, rather than grow bitter against him. Otherwise, why would Ruth have chosen this God to be her own? And the joy of Ruth's confession of faith in God, in turn, must have helped fill the void in Naomi's heart left by the premature departures of her three men.

The hand of God unobtrusively arranged her circumstances, movements, and participation. Indeed, God was the chief participant in the entire story of Ruth and Naomi.

Oh, trust yourself to Jesus
When loved ones pass away,
And life is sad and lonely,
And very dark the way:
Then is the hour for yielding
Entirely to His will;
Then is the time for singing,
"I have my Savior still."
Oh, trust yourself to Jesus
When you are full of care,
For loved ones still refusing
Our blessed hope to share:
Then in the hour of trusting
Our Lord to bring them nigh:
Then is the time for singing,
"He loves them more than I."
—*Unknown*

Things to think about:

1. What kind of resources have you relied upon during devastating times? If you had to go through those trials again, would you change your responses and actions in any way? Explain.

2. Have you known of anyone brought to Christ by the way you or other believers have reacted to losses? What can you learn from their stories?

9

Barzillai: A Senior Who Served God despite Danger

Barzillai shows us how to take our advancing years.
He shows us how to apply our hearts to wisdom
as we number our days. He shows us also . . .
to apply our whole remaining strength,
and our whole remaining time,
to end our days as our days should be ended.
Barzillai having shown us how to live, shows us also
how to die. . . . Barzillai died like the heavenly-minded
man he had always lived.
ALEXANDER WHYTE

BORIS YELTSIN, THE GEORGIAN, AND BARZILLAI, THE Gileadite, two men separated by many centuries and different cultures, have two things in common: Both stood up for toppled rulers, and both refused to conclude that their leaders were guilty of gross mismanagement.

Gorbachev, the former U.S.S.R. president, was put under house arrest, and King David fled Jerusalem for his life. Both men were unjustly and unconstitutionally driven from power. David in Israel and Gorbachev in

Russia were deposed, but neither Barzillai nor Yeltsin said that their rulers were bad for their nations.

Who can forget the picture of Yeltsin standing on a Russian tank protesting Gorbachev's arrest and calling for a general strike? Yeltsin's daring defiance of the coup leaders was similar to the action of Barzillai, who went to David at Mahanaim with supplies so that he could live to fight another day and regain his kingship.

Who was Barzillai (pronounced: Bar-zill-a-i)? We've all read 2 Samuel, but we've tended to glide past Barzillai. He deserves a second look. There are three references to him: 2 Samuel 17:24-29; 19:31-40; 1 Kings 2:7. Psalms 3 and 4, according to the best scholarship, refer to David's experience at Mahanaim, where David went into hiding from Absalom, and there received Barzillai's services and companionship.

Many of the Old Testament oldsters are given honorable mention in the genealogies, but Barzillai, though omitted in the genealogies, got full attention elsewhere. Eighty-year-old Barzillai, an iron man, displayed eight qualities that made him worthy of special mention.

The Quality of Involvement

Barzillai lived in Rogelim, which was in the general vicinity of Mahanaim where David was hiding from Absalom. Knowing that Mahanaim was desolate, Barzillai took it upon himself to organize a food lift to David and his rag-tag army. Two other men were recruited to help: Shobi and Makir.

If he wanted to, Barzillai could have given four reasons for not getting involved:

- He wasn't David's friend. Barzillai lived in a mountainous region far removed from Jerusalem. He had no way of knowing David and could have argued that David neither knew him nor had asked for help.

- He could have used the excuse of age. He could have said, "Why aren't younger men pitching in to help the king? Why should I—I'm old? Let Shobi and Makir do it. I'll stay put."
- He could have used distance as an excuse. Mahanaim was roughly twenty miles south through the mountains. On foot and with pack animals, that was no small matter, especially with warring factions wandering about.
- He could have said, "David must suffer the consequences of mismanagement. After all, when your own son topples you, something must be wrong."

Barzillai wasn't going to wait and see before taking action. He decided to act now and judge later. For, without some intervention, David's future was doomed. So Barzillai went to David's side. Often seniors choose not to get involved in unpopular or seemingly losing causes. They've done their "fair share," "paid their dues."

Some ships that pass disabled vessels in the night are unwilling to answer their distress signals. But others are real heroes. We can guess that David felt as close to Barzillai as a downed F-16 pilot in the Gulf War did to the helicopter rescue pilot.

The Quality of Empathy

We don't know how Barzillai got wind of the coup and David's escape. But when Barzillai did hear of David's plight, his heart went out to him, and his pocketbook was close behind.

Many tried to get close to David for their own personal advantage but forsook him when they felt the heat.

In several psalms David mentioned his anguish over disloyal friends (41:9; 78:57). But the Lord was forever constant (Psalm 4:8).

David's popularity was undoubtedly why some people deserted him. Friendships can turn sour when others feel threatened by our successes. Jealousy is often behind broken friendships. "Friends" become aloof because the awards and acclaim are too much to handle. Attention has been taken away from them, so they break off contact.

David had assets, but they were frozen in Jerusalem. He had an immediate cash-flow problem. Because he left under duress, there was no time to pack. Mahanaim was a desolate place. It had no Holiday Inn or convenience stores. David and his men lacked basic necessities—from beds to bread. Barzillai stepped in with a large donation of supplies.

The Quality of Foresight

The itemized packing list had foods from what we now know as the four basic food groups—cereal/grain, fruits/vegetables, dairy products, meat/fish. Barzillai was intent on not merely supplying sustenance for David and his men, but a balanced diet.

> . . . They also brought wheat and barley, flour and roasted grain, beans and lentils, honey and curds, sheep, and cheese from cows' milk for David and his people to eat. For they said, "The people have become hungry and tired and thirsty in the desert."
> 2 Samuel 17:28-29

The word "roasted" refers to food prepared by dehydration, similar to backpackers' food pouches that don't spoil. Barzillai must have realized that the troops were there for the long haul.

He also anticipated their need for cooking and eating utensils, both small and large (2 Samuel 17:28). The inventory of "bowls" probably referred to large field kettles. "Pottery" referred to cups and pitchers. We can imagine Barzillai supervising the packing to insure that nothing was lost or broken. He probably rode the lead horse as the caravan of supplies moved down the mountain passes to the desolate clearing of Mahanaim.

God raised up Barzillai to give David physical and psychological support. He came to David's rescue. David, a talented king unjustly evicted, received Barzillai's backing. "See how wonderfully God raises up friends for his ministers and people, for their shelter in difficult times."[1] David saw God's hand in the help of the mountain chieftain.

The Quality of Courage

Many assume that heroism evaporates with the onslaught of years, that fright accompanies "the coming of white." But 80-year-old Barzillai did not quake at opposition. He could stand tall without standing scared in support of a worthy leader.

Barzillai knew that if Absalom succeeded in permanently removing David, his father, as king, his own life was endangered. In going to David's side, Barzillai risked his own arrest and execution. But in Barzillai's eyes a quality king deserved backing. Dinsdale T. Young said, "[Barzillai] was not for anyone who might win, but for one who ought to win."[2]

David did not get a delayed or half-hearted donation from Barzillai. He got more than care packages or token attention. In addition, Barzillai wasn't an anonymous benefactor, for he went with the shipment. He risked his own future in securing David's.

Seniors are often described as being full of fear—fearful of heights, fearful of nights, fearful of driving. But 80-year-old Barzillai was fearless, daring to defy the "David-dumpers."

On his 82nd birthday a young photographer said to Sir Winston Churchill, "I hope I may have the privilege of taking your picture when you're one hundred." Sir Winston cheerfully responded, "No reason why you shouldn't, if you continue to look after your health."

The Quality of Generosity

Barzillai was a man of wealth (2 Samuel 19:32). He got rich from the fertile hills, probably as a successful animal husbandman or farmer. Along with wealth came responsibilities, reputation, influence, and possibly a job in local politics. He wanted his money to be used to promote the just cause of David. No expense was spared in getting David restored to his office.

Full support was Barzillai's style. He is a symbol of those many Christian seniors who give generously to God's work. Large bequests and generous gifts from Christian seniors indicate the depth of their feelings, the totality of their dedication, and their determination to keep the causes of Christ not only solvent, but strong. Many Christian seniors reduce their own financial security by making courageous donations for the spread of the gospel.

Today's Barzillais also pitch in, contributing to churches and Christian enterprises by volunteering their expertise. Retired executives, generals, and scientists have donated their time, talent, and energies to jump-start stalled Christian enterprises. Many Christian seniors refuse pay for their efforts and consider it an offering of thanks to God for his goodness down through the years.

Praise God for the Barzillais of the modern church. How much we owe to people of substance who are committed to the gospel and who go the extra mile in helping churches, pastors, colleges, and missions to be strong and to go forward.

> Though troubles assail us, and dangers afright,
> Though friends should all fail us, and foes all unite,
> Yet one thing secures us, whatever betide,
> The promise assures us, "the Lord will provide."
> The birds, without garner or storehouse, are fed;
> From them let us learn to trust God for our bread:
> His saints what is fitting shall ne'er be denied
> So long as 'tis written, "the Lord will provide."
> When Satan assails us to stop up our path,
> And courage all fails us, we triumph by faith.
> He cannot take from us, though oft he has tried,
> This heart cheering promise, "the Lord will provide."
> No strength of our own, and no goodness we claim;
> Yet, since we have known of the Savior's great Name,
> In this our strong tower for safety we hide:
> The Lord is our power, "the Lord will provide."
> —*John Newton*

The Quality of Independence

Barzillai's independence comes across strongly in his second meeting with David, after David was restored to kingship. David invited Barzillai to return with him and to live in Jerusalem as his permanent guest. Barzillai's answer showed a man who appreciated the consideration, but chose to remain where he was.

> How many more years will I live; that I should go up to Jerusalem with the king? I am now eighty years old. Can I tell the difference between what is good and what is not? Can your servant taste what he eats and drinks? Can I still hear the voices of men and women singers? Why should your servant be an added burden to my lord the king? Your servant will cross over the Jordan with the king for a short distance, but why should the king reward me in this way? Let your servant return, that I may die in my own town near the tomb of my father and mother. But here is your servant Kimham. Let him cross over with my lord the king. Do for him whatever pleases you. *2 Samuel 19:34-37*

Barzillai declined David's tempting perks. Cashing in on connections is every politician's dream. Many have aspired to political posts because of the side benefits of winning an election.

Consider two historical instances. During the American Revolution, Silas Deane made deals for personal profit at the expense of his patriotic countrymen.[3] Historians estimate that in 1867 at least $200,000.00 of the 7.2 million it cost to buy Alaska ended up in the pockets of congressmen.[4]

How many seniors would have jumped at the chance of being on David's payroll? Few today would turn down an open-ended invitation to live in or near the White House.

That was one feature that set Barzillai apart from his countrymen. He was not greed-driven. Barzillai did not worship wealth. He could have lived off of "royalties" without writing a word! But Barzillai was independently rich. After all, it took big bucks to feed a king and his army for many months in a remote place.

> Old men are not easily moved. It is difficult to transplant old trees.—*Joseph Parker*

Barzillai showed his independence in his unwillingness to leave the region. Transplanting a countryboy to the city would have taken a twenty-mule team. To confirm to David that no deal could be made, Barzillai noted that he felt an obligation to live out his days in the place where his parents were buried. That was the clincher, for to Jews burial requests were nearly sacred oaths. Recall how Joseph did not want to be buried in Egypt. His body was exhumed and transported back to his homeland. Barzillai could not be coaxed to leave his territory in life or in death.

The Quality of Modesty

Barzillai's listing of senior health problems is impressive; he checked them off as if he were a health-care professional: faltering mental alertness and poor judgment, a lack of appetite and the ability to enjoy food, inability to hear well and to appreciate the arts, and the general nuisance of requiring attendants. If Barzillai actually believed he was giving a thumb-nail sketch of himself, he comes across as a moaner, groaner, and pessimist. Should we take him seriously?

One humorous aspect was his ability to eloquently describe these conditions. That proved his mind was still agile and his wit still active. The logistics of getting all those goods for so many soldiers down the mountain was not a project for a feeble old man. Barzillai was an octogenarian who evidenced a hale old age. Though from the hills, he was certainly not *over* the hill!

It is more than likely that Barzillai's allusion to his ailing old age was a diplomatic way of declining David's offer. Citing health problems would land more softly on the king's ears than, "Well, I'd rather not stay at your palace." Barzillai didn't think of himself as physically finished. Rather he was self-effacing in the interest of graciousness.

The Quality of Spirituality

Appreciation for Barzillai's emergency assistance and enthusiastic loyalty prompted David to present him with a *carte blanche* invitation to live out his days under the bounty and protection of the king. When Barzillai declined, he put in a good word for his son, Kimham. And David did not forget; he made sure that after he died Solomon would provide a place for Kimham in his administration.

David felt a kinship with Barzillai. It went beyond admiration for a helping hand. It went beyond appreciation for his risk-taking and sacrifices. There was a spiritual oneness that came through both in word and deed. The parting of David and Barzillai has the same memorable and moving power as the one between Paul and the Ephesian elders (Acts 20:17-38). Before crossing the Jordan, "The king kissed Barzillai and gave him his blessing, and Barzillai returned to his home."

Only a few verses are dedicated to the important role played by an obscure 80-year-old man. What spirit he showed! In our latter years let us strive to exhibit the same qualities as those found in Barzillai: involvement, empathy, foresight, courage, generosity, independence, modesty, and spirituality.

Things to think about:

1. Have you ever risked your reputation, assets, or life for anyone in serving Christ?

2. What should make you willing to stand for someone who was unjustly treated and cruelly criticized? What has *prevented* you from doing so in past situations?

3. How might the support of Barzillai apply to church and pastoral relations?

10

David: A Senior Who Applauded God

Jesus asked, "How can you believe
if you accept praise from one another?"
JOHN 5:44

The habit of living for the applause of our fellow men
in religious things is deadly.
B. B. WARFIELD

"Let everything that has breath praise the Lord.
Praise the Lord."
PSALM 150:6

D AVID, SWEET SINGER OF ISRAEL AND ITS KING FOR FORTY
years, died at seventy, "having enjoyed long life, wealth
and honor" (1 Chronicles 29:28). The last ten years of his
life, however, were not a cakewalk. Indeed, it was a
rough decade. He sustained the revolt of Absalom, his
son, a three-year famine after his return to power, then
the usurpation of his other son, Adonijah.

David could have moaned and complained to the sky.
But in the last decade of his life, he did not hang up his
harp. He still wrote a significant number of psalms—
between sixty-three and eighty. David's faith was severe-

ly tested in his senior years. But his trust in God showed a titanium tenacity.

What about that period of his life when he relinquished his title and passed on his kingship to Solomon? The words of David in 2 Samuel 23:1 are recorded as his last words. But were they his very last words or his last *official* words? I believe that David's deathbed charge to Solomon (2 Kings 2:1ff) was followed by his last psalm.

An Ending Psalm to Life

Psalm 72 constitutes David's last psalm. It has the superscription, "Of Solomon." Then at the very end of the psalm it reads, "This concludes the prayers of David son of Jesse." There appears to be a conflicting claim to authorship.

Several explanations of this seeming contradiction have been proposed but, in my opinion, John Calvin's explanation is still the best. His view was that Psalm 72 was David's dictation to his son, Solomon, as he approached death.

> After carefully weighing all, I incline to the view that David uttered this prayer as he was dying, and that it was put into the form of a Psalm by his son, Solomon, that the memory thereof might never perish. As Solomon took the argument from his father, and only clothed it in the garb of poetry, we may regard David as the principal author.[1]

Psalm 72 was both Solomon's psalm and David's prayer. A person's last words in life often reflect the way he lived and how he thought. Few people will equivocate, vacillate, or pontificate while they are dying. Final words can be significant.[2]

David's doxology in Psalm 72:18-19 reflects his royal orientation and his real spiritual attitude. These two verses are David's last private words. And what are they about? Judge for yourself:

> Praise be to the LORD God, the God of Israel, who alone does marvelous deeds. Praise be to his glorious name forever; may the whole earth be filled with his glory. Amen and Amen.

If Solomon had to take down David's last whispered words, he was probably immobile. He could hardly raise his head, let alone his hand to write. Even at the end David's devotion bubbled up and broke out in discernible words. Deep faith should never be speechless. If we really have convictions, we should be able to articulate them. David did.

In Old Testament times the elevation of kings was greeted with applause. King Josiah, for instance, was surrounded by subjects, staff, and special guests at his coronation. The official record of the ceremony says, "They anointed him, and the people clapped their hands and shouted, 'Long live the king!' " (2 Kings 11:12).

Earlier, when David became king, he was given similar applause. Every king heard applause at the start of his reign. But David, in his dying, wanted to hear not applause for himself but for God. He gave God sustained applause, just as England's Welsh king, Henry the 5th, left life saying, "Laud be to God, even there my life shall end" (*Henry 5th*, Act 4, Sc. 5, 1. 235).

In sharp contrast was the closing scene in the life of powerful Caesar Augustus (27 B.C.-14 A.D.), the ruler of Judea when Jesus was born. Caesar Augustus lived for applause. When he entered his box at the amphitheatre, he received a standing ovation. When he came to die, according to historian Seutonious, Augustus asked his friends "whether he had fitly gone through the play of life . . . [and if so] begged for their applause like an actor on the point of leaving the stage."[3]

Giving Due Praise to God

Applause is appropriate and invigorating when an actor finishes a play and leaves the stage. But sincere appreciation can pass into self-glory without much effort.

David died exhorting Solomon and us to give God all the glory. He did not speak about his accomplishments. He did not ask that his deeds be recited. He made no mention of his just rule and excellent record. Rather, he talked of God's wonders.

As for his own notoriety? David was content to let it fade. He did not turn to friends for compliments or to his family for praise. God the Creator, God the Governor, God the Judge, and God the Savior occupied David's attention, and were part of his meditation. David's love for God was very much alive; self-exaltation was dead.

Even in David's last official, public words in 2 Samuel 23, he acknowledges God's role in the fate of Israel:

> The God of Israel spoke, the Rock of Israel said to me: "When one rules over men in righteousness, when he rules in the fear of God, he is like the light of morning at sunrise on a cloudless morning, like the brightness after rain that brings the grass from the earth."
>
> Is not my house right with God? Has he not made with me an everlasting covenant, arranged and secured in every part? Will he not bring to fruition my salvation and grant me my every desire?

Here lay one of the world's most renowned kings; his wealth would be exceeded only by that of his son after him. He was lauded as a great warrior and as a poet. Yet hardly a phrase ever came from his pen that did not somehow connect God to lives of people, nations, and the world. David knew to whom praise was due.

Sometimes relatives will try to encourage the dying with expressions of appreciation and praise. Indeed, Solomon may have poured out such things to his father. If this is true, there is no indication of it in David's response, in his ending words. He was preoccupied with honoring and praising the God whom he had loved and served all those years, the God who had cared for him and been his strength.

Self-praise detracts from a Christian's life of faith. Like David we should desire God's exaltation in all things. Jesus could not make headway with the Pharisees because they were hungering for praise from their friends (John 5:44). When self-love blares, God's praise is muted. Heaven's occupation is in giving all glory to God (Revelation 5:13).

We cannot begin to duplicate David's exploits or match his character. We will be frustrated by trying to rival his poetic gifts, but we can be like him in enthusiastically and energetically praising God with all our strength and to our last breath.

Alexander Solzhenitsyn described a forced, mandatory, standing ovation for Stalin at a district conference in Moscow:

The small hall echoed with "stormy applause, rising to an ovation." For three minutes, four minutes, five minutes . . . palms were getting sore and raised arms were already aching. And the older people were panting from exhaustion. Who would dare to be the first to stop? NVK [KGB] men were standing in the hall applauding and watching to see who would quit first. . . . The applause went on six, seven, eight minutes . . . nine minutes.[4]

When praise of others is coaxed or coerced, the human exaltation is hollow. But there was no such stilted quality to the praise David offered to his Lord. His words of adoration sprang spontaneously from a deep relationship and from a gratefully received, divine forgiveness.

Praise Takes Us Beyond Ourselves

In his last prayer, David looked ahead to an unusual heir:

> May his name endure forever; may it continue as long as the sun. All nations will be blessed through him, and they will call him blessed. *Psalm 72:17*

David had in fact glimpsed Jesus, the coming King, David's true successor. David himself would not fulfill Israel's need and the world's hopes. Only a divine Messiah could fulfill the goal. The ideal king "lay beyond the capabilities of the Davidic dynasty, or any of its representatives."[5]

David's anticipation of the Messiah showed that he recognized the limitations of his own reign; his power could not bring about any ultimate good. Only in this admission could he glorify God. We, too, must admit that we are sinners, distanced from God and totally dependent on him. Then we can affirm David's praise of God—"who alone does wondrous things."

David did not have his eyes fixed on his own kingship. Although he had reached the summit of human achievement and deserved tributes from his contemporaries, these were all empty and temporary expressions of appreciation. David's final meditation of God's magnificent rule was a permanent reminder to Solomon (and to us) of the necessity to ascribe praise, honor, wisdom, might, and glory to God before we meet him in the next world.

A Life of Praise Leads to Peace and Joy

A brief scanning of the book of Psalms reveals how much of David's (and the other psalmists') praise grew out of their observance of the natural world. Creation is glorious. So watching the birds outside our window provides us thoughts of God's faithful provision and protection of one of the least of God's creatures. Observing the gradual unfolding of fragile flowers along the house is space enough for us to reflect on God's inventiveness and infinitude. What God makes grow, we can photograph and paint, but we cannot duplicate. "God alone does wondrous things!"

From a Christian viewpoint, however, the most magnificent of God's great works is the recovery, rescue, and restoration of sinners. The re-creation of fallen humans requires *divine* power. Our cleansing, our being put right with God, and our heavenly peace are not products of human effort, ingenuity, and perseverance. They are the recreation of Jesus Christ, applied to our souls by the power of his shed blood and resurrection.

God, who puts us right with himself, puts us in tune with his purposes, and our praise of him is an expected consequence. By his liberating Spirit we are enabled to enter into our homes, our yards, our churches with praise, freely and gladly. Have we become so preoccupied with our situations, troubles, decisions, and needs that we have forgotten to lift up our hearts in glorifying God?

David wanted God's glory to be witnessed and adored by all people. He encouraged his son, Israel's next king, to live rightly before God, to trust God as David had. What a vision for the world! He was totally captivated by the underlying goodness and mercy of God. David longed that others would rejoice in the Lord. God's wondrous workings begun in us will influence and encourage others.

David's greater son, Christ, has made us his personal concern. Lean your full weight upon the strong Son of God and thank him for his pardoning generosity. Do not feebly and faintly utter praise to God. Dying David had no stamina of voice to give vigorous speech, yet in his weakness he used sturdy words. One rule of thumb emerges: Worship reaches its zenith in our gratitude to God.

Like David, many seniors can look back on a life blessed by God. Life has been full and the moments have been packed with all sorts of happiness. God's blessings and bounty are evident everywhere in our families, in our careers, in our accomplishments. And through it all we worship our God who does wondrous things.

Choosing Our Audience

Can we see David's viewpoint? Those who cannot may not be playing to God but to society. Keith Miller, an awakened layman in an established denomination, found that many people were not keen on having Christ-centered lives and God-glorifying emphases. He tried to introduce God's glory in a tangible way but was rebuffed.

One day he got an idea from the former Oklahoma football coach, Bud Wilkerson. Bud asked Keith to sit in to watch the game film. As he sat with the players, Keith noticed that they were not the least interested in the noisy crowd and its reactions.

These boys are unconsciously playing the game to a different audience and it freed them from the franticness of the crowd. . . . This idea came as a profound turning point for me in trying to live the Christian life.[6]

Miller thought to use the same principle back at church. He thought it worth a try to get an egotistical bunch of church leaders to live for Christ. But he realized that could not be done unless he was truly living for Christ himself. Step by step, day after day, he was ". . . starting to play [his] life to a different audience—to the living Christ."

In his better moments, especially his final hours, King David played to the audience of God. His praise was the result of learning to know and please God.

Too many folks are like Mr. By-Ends in Bunyan's *Pilgrim's Progress.* Mr. By-Ends and his wife, Lady Feigning, thrived on public praise. Jointly, they said, "We love much to walk with [Christian] in the street, if the sun shines and people applaud him."

Living totally for God in our society will not get us pats on the back and plaques on the wall. We should not go to church, read our Bibles, visit the sick, or join in prayers in order to be seen and to be complimented. The impulse should grow out of our relationship with Christ, and the practice should be maintained out of genuine devotion. These activities do become habit-forming, but the habit is generated by a spiritual force.

God multiplies years and provides extended life. Life is able to rise above mere existence when the Lord is central in our thinking, the one to whom we give all praise. David left life vigorously praising God. Do we begin and end our days with prime attention to the Lord? May David inspire us to praise the Lord with effort and enjoyment. His words can teach us how to worship energetically:

> May his name endure forever; may his name increase as long as the sun shines; and let men bless themselves by him; let all nations call him blessed. Blessed be the LORD God, the God of Israel, who alone works wonders. And blessed be his glorious name forever; and may the whole earth be filled with his glory. *Psalm 72:17-19,* NASB

Things to think about:

1. What part do you think applause should have in church services?

2. Do you think David's focus on God's achievements amount to false modesty? How did David's practice fit with Jesus' warning in John 5:44?

3. What forms can "applause" take? List some means we have of giving praise to God.

11

Solomon: A Senior Poet Who Gave a Pep Talk

Out of dust Thy Word creative
formed the house in which I dwell,
and the wonders of its being
neither tongue nor pen can tell.
Flesh and blood and brain together,
in a unity sublime,
Thou didst make to be thy dwelling
in this sunlit veil of time.

UNKNOWN

Some day the silver cord will break,
And I no more as now shall sing;
But O, the joy when I shall wake
Within the palace of the King!
Some day my earthly house will fall,
I cannot tell how soon 'twill be,
But this I know—my All in All
Has now a place in Heav'n for me.

FANNY J. CROSBY

BEVERAGE COMMERCIALS USE BEACH SCENES TO CONVEY A party atmosphere. Glamour, good times, glitz, and go-for-it attitudes pervade images of the upwardly mobile. The youth market gets special attention because it is more open to buying into the changing fashion market.

Increasingly, seniors are also receiving advertising attention, because manufacturers recognize the growing senior market. Advertisers appeal to the positive features of good nutrition, regular exercise, simple pleasures, and family togetherness.

By the same token, senior anxieties (fixed incomes and uncertain health conditions) get plenty of airtime, too. Health insurance, exercise equipment, blood-pressure kits, security systems, and medical alert gadgets are being peddled to those predisposed to shop by phone.

Seniors are encouraged to plug into technological benefits. Discrimination against aging (ageism) is decried. Senior lobbies now demand equal treatment under the law for those in their latter years. Retirees unashamedly flex their poll power. Magazines such as *Modern Maturity* carry ads designed to alert seniors to better products, suppliers, and services.

But where can seniors look for materials that speak to their spiritual lives? Periodicals such as *Guideposts* give occasional mention of older, God-centered people and their stories. But most publications seriously neglect the spiritual dimension of seniors' lives. For that kind of information, the Bible is still the best place to look.

Ecclesiastes is commonly thought to be written by King Solomon. The author was a son of David and a king. But the name is never given, so the book's authorship has long been the subject of debate.[1]

There are some aspects of Ecclesiastes that fit Solomon to a "T" and therefore make a strong case for him being the writer. Solomon, for instance, enjoyed prosperity. He was a person of prominence and of political power. He had innumerable advantages and access to excellence in every phase of life. He was wealthy and had a full life of experiences from which to share.

Solomon was active in his senior years. He kept experimenting and expanding his experiences. Ecclesiastes reflects a man who maximized his enjoyments and had the means to cater to mature ambitions and tastes. He had the best of the world and enjoyed life to the fullest with its frills and thrills.

Ecclesiastes is a book worth pondering. It offers a no-holds-barred approach to living. Sometimes it is bitter and brusque. Hearing from a person of experience how life should be and how it in fact is remains the distinctive characteristic of this book.

The book concludes with a grand and graphic poem. The opening section (11:9-10; 12:1) is addressed to adolescent youth. The author identifies with the younger generation in its capacity to enjoy life. He also warns and gives perspective. Without squelching youthful spontaneity, the author reminds his readers to be realistic. Youth is not all there is to life.

Putting Youth in Perspective

The poetic portion is not exclusively addressed to seniors, but apparently authored by one. The exhortation, "Remember your Creator in the days of your youth" (12:1) is primarily aimed at young people, warning them of their limited opportunity ("before the days of trouble come").

The time to really remember is in adolescence. The memory must be cultivated then, for as the following description shows, there comes a time when memory does not work. Solomon points out an irony—that adolescents can suffer a loss of memory! Remembering God is what many young people forget. And forgetting

God makes life utterly futile even when we are young and physically powerful.

Solomon's pep talk to youth was also a poem on aging. Consider it King Solomon's testimony to life as it is and life as it should be. As a senior, Solomon had no worries about his pension drying up. He could go on spending sprees without calculating for monthly bills. Even powerful medieval kings probably were not as well off as Solomon in all his glory.

> I made great works; I built houses and planted vineyards for myself; I made myself gardens and parks . . . I made myself pools from which to water the forest of growing trees . . . I got singers . . . I kept my heart from no pleasure. *Ecclesiastes 2:4-10,* RSV

Despite these conveniences, comforts, and cozy circumstances, Solomon thought of other dwellings, homes of special importance. He alluded to three types of homes.

The House We Fill

Have you seen the maternity sweat shirts that read, "New Baby under Construction"? Homes are made, not born. But humans are both made and born. When placed on the earth we come with all the necessary plumbing, pumps, wiring, switches, fixtures, parts, and rooms. Yet God lets us fill the most important vacant space.

The mind is one room we must fill. We are born without knowledge. Our brains come unfurnished. But what kind of thoughts do we let lodge there? Sir Arthur Conan Doyle, author of the Sherlock Holmes mysteries, didn't leave us in much doubt when he said, "a man's brain originally is like a little empty attic. And you have to stock it with such furniture as you choose."

> I have a house inside of me
> A house that people seldom see:
> It has a door through which none pass
> And windows, but they're not of glass.
> "Where do you live?" ask folks I meet,
> And then I say, "On such a street."
> But still I know what's really me
> Lives in a house folks never see.
> —*Unknown*

Solomon said in Proverbs 24:3-4 that "By wisdom a house is built . . . through knowledge its rooms are filled with rare and beautiful treasure." Israel showed poor judgment in departing from the revealed knowledge of God. Jeremiah asked, "How long shall your wicked thoughts lodge within you?" (Jeremiah 4:14, NKJV). Solomon challenged young people to cherish, remember, and rely on God.

Much study can weary the body (Ecclesiastes 12:12), but the knowledge of God can revive the spirit. Solomon's tale-end commendation of the knowledge of God was, doubtless, the result of having forgotten God in his own youth. He regretted having wasted so much time and energy on foreign gods.

Ideas are mind furnishings. Many people love Ethan Allen furniture, but, ironically, the philosophy of the man Ethan Allen was dangerous.

Ethan Allen was a famous early American. One of the leaders of the American Revolution, he wrote pamphlets to promote his political views. He was also a deist.

As a deist, he did not believe that the Bible should be the final authority over people's lives, but that they should have authority over the Bible. He wrote, among other things, a booklet entitled, *Reason, the Only Oracle of*

Man (1784). In it he opposed the doctrine of original sin. He didn't regard Scripture as God's self-revelation or as authoritative.

Deism taught that God made the world but then took his hands off it and let it run by natural laws without interference.

Can such ideas about God coexist with what we learn from Scripture? We get particular about what furnishings we have in our homes, so why aren't we particular about the ideas we admit into our minds? Ideas that look nice may be a source of false comfort. Deistic ideas put God at a distance, and to many that is a consoling thought. But the Bible presents a God who is involved in history and our lives.

It is not enough to catalog facts in our heads as if they were nonfunctional pieces of information. Of course, our brains have a remarkable storage capacity. Each human brain has a cavernous chain of crisscrossed, recessed chambers that hold an enormous amount of information. The incredible, almost infinite, creative and cognitive powers we possess deserve something better than tidbit facts, splinters of gossip, and passing headlines. Our minds are made in God's image. They warrant magnificent and majestic ideas. The knowledge of God should live in our "upper story" and direct our lives.

What thoughts control us? How deeply has a scriptural world view entered our thinking? Do we allow biblical truths into the hall and a few small rooms? Some make room in the library or the dining room but outlaw biblical ethics in the family room. We may exclude him from the closets, basement, and back rooms, where we hide offensive things. Solomon warned the young that God will bring every thought, word, and deed into account. Similarly, St. Paul advised that God's judgment would disclose the hidden things of darkness (1 Corinthians 4:5).

Robert Munger developed the idea of Jesus requesting access to the various rooms of our lives. Jesus leaves every room he lives in better, cleaning as he goes. Recognizing Jesus' ability to rearrange and improve the various compartments of his life, Munger prayed:

"Lord, is there any chance that You would take over the management of the whole house and operate it for me as You did that closet? Would You take the responsibility to keep my life what it ought to be?" . . . [Christ replied,] "Certainly, that is what I want to do. You cannot be a victorious Christian in your own strength. That is impossible. Let Me do it through you and for you." . . . [Munger continued,] "Lord, You have been a guest and I have been the host. From now on I am going to be the servant. You are going to be the Lord."[2]

Coming to the place where we want God to order our lives is not easy. It's not enough to give Jesus an occasional tour of our minds. We must allow him to exercise his lordship, putting him in charge of our moments and our thoughts. We need to recognize him as the chief resident, as our true host and owner. We don't need to dread the rearrangement of our private thoughts and priorities. We should expect that certain ideas must be moved out so that Christ-honoring, God-glorifying thoughts can take their places.

By the time Ecclesiastes was written, Solomon's days of flirtation with false gods were over. He had come to renewed appreciation of the God of his father, King David. From what he says throughout Ecclesiastes, it is apparent that some of this renewed interest in God was due to the trial and error, the unfulfillment of his own life, even with its riches and self-indulgence. Perhaps his disappointments led him once again to the writings of Moses and others who had recorded Israel's history with the Lord. We can only guess about the process that brought him to the wisdom and reflection found in Ecclesiastes.

If Jesus came to your house to spend a day or two,
If He came unexpectedly, I wonder what you would do.
Oh, I know you'd give your nicest room to such an
   honored guest,
And all the food you'd serve to Him would be the very best,
And you would keep assuring Him you're glad to have
   Him there,
That serving Him in your own home is joy beyond
   compare. . . .
I wonder if the Savior spent a day or two with you,
Would you go right on doing the things you always do?
Would life for you continue as it does from day to day?
Would you keep right on saying the things you always say?
Would you be glad to have Him stay forever, on and on,
Or would you sigh with great relief when He at last was gone?
—Lois Blanchard

The House We Live In

Near the end of his life, John Quincy Adams, our sixth President, said to Daniel Webster, "I inhabit a weak, frail, decayed tenement, battered by the winds, and broken in upon by storms, and from all I can learn, the Landlord does not intend to repair."

Our bodies are much like buildings. And the signs of aging in the body are similar to the signs of decline in a building.

For the majority . . . [old age is] like living in a house that's in increasing need of repairs. The plumbing doesn't work right any more. There are bats in the attic. Cracked and dusty, the windows are hard to see through, and there's a lot of creaking and groaning in bad weather. The exterior could use a coat of paint . . . The eighty-year-old body can be in precarious shape yet the spirit within as full of beans as ever.[3]

Ecclesiastes 12:3-7 is a classic description of aging. It talks about various maladies that affect old body parts:

> . . . The sun and the light
> and the moon and the stars grow dark,
> and the clouds return after the rain;
> When the keepers of the house tremble,
> and the strong men stoop,
> When the grinders cease because they are few,
> and those looking through the windows grow dim;
> When the doors to the street are closed
> and the sound of grinding fades;
> when men rise up at the sound of birds,
> but all their songs grow faint;
> when men are afraid of heights
> and of dangers in the streets;
> when the almond tree blossoms
> and the grasshopper drags himself along
> and desire no longer is stirred.

In this poetic treatment we find probable allusion to eyesight fading, trembling limbs, stooping backs, worn out teeth, insomnia (rising with the birds), impaired hearing, loss of balance, graying hair (blossoms on the almond tree), halted walking like that of a wounded grasshopper, and decreased sexual drive.[4]

Psychologist Stanley Hall has regarded this elaborate analogy as "the most pessimistic description of old age ever written."[5] Is it a litany of laments? Are these literary expressions meant to pull down the shades, inject gloom, and cause a person to be depressed about his health?

First, keep in mind that the purpose of these words was to jolt the indifferent youth who brazenly avoid, neglect, and forget God (12:1). Young persons, who normally have few aches or pains, may feel they are immortal because of their physical vigor and virility. This passage is designed to inject them with realism.

With all our present cosmetic helps, miniature hearing aids, and medications, many signs of aging are not so evident today. But anyone who has lived much past his or her twenties and thirties can relate to the effects time has on the body. Even for those in good health the changes are perceptible; we know that we certainly won't dwell in these "houses" forever.

A man in his nineties went to a general practitioner with a knee problem. After examining the man's knee, the physician said, "What is your age?" The man replied, "Ninety, Doc." "Well," continued the physician, "at your age what can you expect?" The puzzled senior replied: "Doc, I expect you to fix my knee. My other knee is the same age and that works fine!"

Secondly, some playful optimism pervades the description. Jacques Ellul has pointed out some notes of hope in the passage. A few light touches modulate the description of how a person's sturdiness dwindles and darkens toward the end of earthly existence. The birds still sing, the almond tree blooms, and the grasshopper is no longer something to fear, destroying and devastating all vegetations in its path. Ellul reminds us that in the Old Testament the blooming almond tree represented hope, gratitude, vigilance, and activity. "He interlaces all these final images with subtle suggestions of hope, like arrows that draw our gaze toward a different end."[6]

Solomon would have appreciated Phyllis McGinley's knee-slapping jingle describing her 70th birthday:

> Seventy is wormwood;
> Seventy is gall.
> But it is better to be 70,
> Than not alive at all.

The point of the passage is to remind us to utilize our time to glorify God by remembering him and by living for him. Remembering our Creator involves reflection on our creaturehood. Grooming ourselves for God's use should occupy our youth. Piety is important in the sunset years, of course, but it should begin in adolescence when our powers are at their energetic peak.

The sixfold repetition of the word "before" emphasizes the urgency of living for the Lord:

before the time of trouble
before the dimness and darkness of age
before the arrival of storms
before the silver cord is snapped
before the pitcher is shattered
before our light dust returns to the heavier earth.

Side with the Lord early in life. Don't wait until strength fails, the mind slows, and joints stiffen. Don't wait until it's too late to catch up, too painful to kneel in prayer, too taxing to read, and too demanding to travel. Now is the day of salvation. Encourage young people to give their best days to the Lord. "Remember now your Creator in the days of your youth."

Abuse of our bodies reduces our capacity to focus on God. Ceaseless motion without reflection will waste our energies and shorten our opportunities. Those who contend there is nothing to eternity often end up making an eternity of nothing.

The Home We Are Going To

Solomon didn't need to cut corners when he built homes. They were sturdy, ample, and ornate. He used precious metals and gems for finishing touches.

Lavish homes were as prized in the Old Testament as they are today. Jeremiah said, "Shame on the man who says, 'I will build a spacious house with airy roof chambers, set windows in it, panel it with cedar and paint it with vermilion!' If your cedar is more splendid, does that prove you are a king?" (Jeremiah 22:15-16, NEB).

Solomon referred to life after death as going home: ". . . man goes to his eternal home . . ." (12:5). Can we assume that we will have a roof over our heads after death? Scripture sometimes refers to hell as wandering and ceaseless roaming. If we refuse fellowship with God here, the hereafter will not be "going home" but going to a strange and unfamiliar place, to a hovel instead of a home, to a matchbox instead of an estate of many rooms.

The God-oriented believer can be assured of a home with God in the future. "Now at last God has his dwelling place among men!" (Revelation 21:3, NEB). Some people cannot look forward to that.

Christians do not need to panic when their bodies fall apart. We will not be homeless. Our powers may dwindle, our frames droop and shrink, our appetites wane, our movements cease, and our hearts stop. But though the outward body perishes, the inward person is being readied for a new place, a reserved home. Jesus has gone ahead to prepare us a place, ready for occupancy. We will not be spiritually homeless at death, for God has given forethought to our eternal dwelling.

The human body is a wonderful home and we hate to vacate it. We would prefer to stay with our family and friends where the fellowship has been good. But there is an expanded version of God's goodness ahead. "To die is gain," said St. Paul (Philippians 1:21). No matter how well we have managed the property God has loaned to us, we must eventually move on to a new home. We will not be locked out of heaven, for Jesus Christ is the key to our eternal residence.

> You tell me that I'm getting old
> I tell you that's not so!
> The house I live in is all worn out,
> And that of course I know.
> It's been in use a long, long time
> And weathered many a gale.
> I'm really not surprised to find
> It's getting somewhat frail.
> The color is changing on the roof
> And the windows are getting dim,
> The steps are now quite well worn
> Their appearance no longer trim.
> The foundation is not as steady
> As once it used to be.
> Yes, my house is getting shaky,
> But my house is just not me!
> A few short years can't make me old,
> I feel I'm in my youth
> Eternity lies just ahead
> A life of joy and truth.
> I'm going to live forever there,
> And I think it will be grand.

You tell me that I'm getting old,
You just don't understand.
The dweller in my little house
Is bright and young today,
Just starting out on life
That lasts a great eternal day.
You only see the outside,
Which is all that most folks see.
You tell me that I'm getting old.
You've mixed my house with me.
—*Dora Johnson, adapted by author*

Things to think about:

1. Who are some of the young people in your life for whom you have special concern? How can you challenge them, as the author of Ecclesiastes challenged the youth of his day?

2. Which experiences in your life point to God's faithfulness and the satisfaction of walking with him? Consider leaving a permanent record of your faith by asking to have a videotape made, or write it on paper, or use an audiotape. Plan how you can leave a legacy of faith to the generations after you—like Solomon!

12

Zechariah: A Senior Who Faced Frustration

They say in Switzerland that the Swiss climbers have a rope, the strands of which at the center are the strongest and are capable of holding up a man even if all the edges of the rope have worn off. The inmost strands are the strongest. I have found that to be true in Christian experience. Many of the strands of my life have been broken by [my] stroke, for I can no longer preach and I cannot write as my eyesight is so poor that I cannot see my own writing. I can only dictate into a tape recorder. The things that were dear to me, for the time being, are broken. The innermost strands belonging to the Kingdom and the Person of Jesus and my experience of him holds me as much as the total rope, for the innermost strands are the strongest. I need no outer props to hold up my faith, for my faith holds me. Though I do not possess my faith, it possesses me.

E. STANLEY JONES

ZECHARIAH WAS AN OLD MAN, BUT HE CONTINUED TO work as a priest. Should he have retired? Numbers 8:24-25 indicates that Levites or assistant priests, who had the responsibility of lifting, caring, and setting up the heavy tabernacle furniture, were to retire at age fifty. But Zechariah was not a Levite priest, and the need for furniture movers disappeared once there was a permanent temple.

At this time there was no retiring age for a priest.[1] "A priest served as long as he was able."[2] His wife, Elizabeth, also up in years, probably didn't want him to retire. Why? Like wives today, when men retire the wives get half as much money and twice as much husband! Giving up the joy of serving in God's temple would have been quite an emotional loss, quite possibly resulting in an unhappy husband.

Fortunately, for Zechariah, he did not come under the U.S. Social Security Act of 1933, which set a retirement age at sixty-five. If he had retired at sixty-five, he would have missed out on the greatest event in his life—offering the incense at the temple.

Transition to retirement can be traumatic. After the joviality of the office party, after the last timecard is punched, the reality of our new circumstances sets in. Post-retirement thoughts can be laced with agonizing regrets and painful withdrawals. Counselor Edgar N. Jackson writes:

> Retirement often causes a crisis of confidence. If a person has done useful work and enjoyed doing it, he may feel he has experienced a form of death when he retires.[3]

Have you ever noticed that the Old Testament mindset did not make retirement a goal? I think part of the reason people lived longer was that they kept busy—tending sheep, harvesting grain, and making wine.

A prominent citizen nearing eighty-seven years old was asked by a news reporter what exercises he did to keep fit. "My boy," the oldster said, "when you're pushing eighty-seven, that's all the exercise you need."

People in the church today tend to have a low view of the aging. Compared to the Old Testament outlook, we minimize the value of age. At best, some think of ministry *to* the aging. Others more diplomatically speak of ministry *with* the aging. Scripture, however, looks upon a ministry *from* the aging.[4]

Ageism is a prejudice against a person because of his or her age. Despair is self-inflicted ageism. Scripture does not tell us Nicodemus's age, but his question to Jesus reflected his own despair as a senior: "How can a man be born [again] when he is old?" (John 3:4). Nicodemus felt victimized by his age. Leon Morris wrote, "He may have been thinking that the past grips us with an all too firm grasp. I am what I am today because of the nature with which I was born and then what all my yesterdays have done to me."[5]

Accumulated skepticism is not too great an obstacle to the recreative power of God. Seniors can also be reborn of God's Spirit. New life in an old body is paradoxical, but not impossible. Zechariah and Elizabeth knew the spiritual vitality that Nicodemus longed to have.

The Holy Spirit inspired Zechariah to draw near to God as a priest. Gereontologists can't quite understand how conversion and continued consecration contribute to good health and long life.

Physiologically, Zechariah may have been more fit than most for his age. After all, biological aging is not uniform, according to medical findings. "Some older men remain capable into their 80s of original thinking and cogent decision making."[6] Zechariah is an inspiration to all senior citizens to keep at their vocations or avocations as long as they are able.

Handel conducted the oratorio *Elijah* at the age of seventy-five. Thomas Edison was still busy in his New Jersey lab at age eighty-four. Think what the world would have missed if these men had quit at sixty-five!

Now a large number of corporation heads are directed by men past their seventies. In 1981, the *New York Times* listed twenty-nine men over age seventy who were chief executives of large corporations.[7]

Volunteer workers from the senior set are welcomed both in the religious and secular areas. More companies, schools, churches, and social services are tapping into the work pool of retirees, benefiting both those who give and those who receive.

Zechariah Was Undaunted by His Age

Zechariah epitomized Psalm 92:14-15:

> They will still bear fruit in old age. They will stay fresh and green, proclaiming, "The Lord is upright; He is my Rock, and there is no wickedness in Him."

Many Americans resist being "put out to pasture." An unwanted early retirement can leave some people bitter, cynical, and chronically depressed. Early retirement can be cruel. After all, why should one-third of a man's life be considered expendable? As far back as 1974, a Harris poll revealed that nearly one third of the nation's retirees said they would still be working if they were able.[8]

Zechariah lived with Scripture sounding in his ears. He and his wife wanted to be useful to God. And he recognized that his longevity was a gift from God: "The fear of the LORD adds length to life" (Proverbs 10:27). A woman, aged 113, made the following comment to former President Reagan when he called her up to congratulate her on her birthday. When asked the secret to her long life, she replied, "You can't add it yourself. God has to add it."

At the time of Zechariah's story, because of the huge number of priests—about 18,000—there was no guarantee that a priest would have the privilege of presiding at a temple service. The 18,000 priests were divided into twenty-four sections. The priest in each section who would have the privilege of performing duties was chosen by lot. "It was quite possible that many a priest would never have the privilege of burning incense all his life; but if the lot did fall on any priest, that day was the greatest day in all his life, the day he longed for and dreamed of."[9]

Zechariah had won a sort of priestly "Lotto." He was chosen not to win money but to get a rare chance to serve in the temple. It was a once-in-a-lifetime privilege. He was overjoyed. It was during the evening offering of incense that the angel of the Lord, Gabriel, confronted Zechariah during his prayers. He had a startling message. He told Zechariah that despite his age and that of his wife they would have a son. The child would be filled with the Holy Spirit from his birth and he would become a prophet who would prepare Israel for the coming of the Messiah.

Zechariah had given up hope that their prayers for a child would be answered. By all calculations, Elizabeth had passed childbearing years. So his reaction was disbelief: "I am an old man and my wife is well along in years."

Zechariah Was Frustrated

Zechariah wanted to be a father, but for most of his adult life that joy was denied him and Elizabeth. Zechariah and Elizabeth lived "by the book," and their "book" was the Old Testament. Luke points out that Zechariah and

Elizabeth were righteous before God. In the Old Testament children were viewed as God's blessing upon a marriage, and to be childless was to be in disgrace.

Childlessness continues to be a disappointment to couples. Many resort to expensive experimental procedures to reverse nature, so great is their desire to have children of their own. The case of Zechariah's and Elizabeth's childlessness is included to comfort those who think their circumstances mean that God is angry with them. Godliness does not exempt us from everyday frustrations. The inability to have children is a complex problem. We should not blame ourselves, nor blame God, for his reasons are inscrutable.

In a sense, many of our deepest longings remain unfulfilled. No matter how full our days, we can't enjoy everything there is in life.

> To leave unseen so many a glorious sight,
> To leave so many lands unvisited,
> To leave so many worthiest books unread,
> Unrealised so many visions bright;—
> Oh, wretched yet inevitable spite
> Of our brief span, that we must yield our breath,
> And wrap us in the unfeeling soil of death,
> So much remaining of improved delight.
> —*Unknown*

The Old Testament helped Zechariah and Elizabeth to accept their status of being childless. They understood that God was almighty and able to do anything; he was in control of the world. It is only when we object to God running the world that our frustrations become unmanageable and we cannot become reconciled to our circumstances. We should learn to say, "Disappointments are his appointments."

Zechariah doubted Gabriel's announcement. He had resigned himself to having no children.

Luke, I believe, included this story of the reversal of nature, not to give older couples unrealistic hopes of altering nature's reproductive course but to remind us that God is sovereign and that no obstacle is too great for him to overcome. Even our unbelief cannot deter God when he sets out to accomplish something. The story reminds us that our lives can be fruitful beyond what we or others think.

Childlessness has its frustrations. Aging has its own frustrations, and growing old can be vexing. The person we see in the mirror is not the person of years ago.

How do we know we are old? We know we are old when our knees buckle, but our belts don't. We know we are old when the question crosses our minds when we are tying our shoes, "Is there anything else I can do while I am down here?" We know we are old when our backs go out more than we do. We know we are old when we turn off the lights for economic, not romantic reasons.—*Unknown*

Because of his unbelief Zechariah became speechless. At the time, Zechariah's inability to speak was attributed to a visionary's temporary trance. But Zechariah's dumbness lasted the full term of his wife's pregnancy. It was only at John's birth, when Zechariah could write his new son's name, that he was able to speak. The length of his speechlessness meant he suffered more than simple shock. What he experienced was like a partial stroke.

Strokes can be more frustrating than infertility. Strokes impair our mobility. Often speech and vision are lost or labored.[10]

E. Stanley Jones, the famous Methodist evangelist, lived a high-energy life until the age of eighty-seven. But he was struck down with a disabling stroke on December 7, 1971. Like Zechariah, there were months before he could return to speaking. He lived to reflect upon his stroke, and what he wrote may help those who have gone through the same emergency. Here is part of what he wrote in his last book, *The Divine Yes.*

I looked forward to a gentle descent into my nineties and perhaps beyond with nothing but gratitude for what God has wrought, for I have watched him do it rather than doing it myself. I had endeavored to be a faithful and humble witness to Christ in every situation. Then suddenly: Bang! I found myself and my future apparently in ruins. My means of locomotion were shattered, and I could not recognize my own voice on a dictaphone. The only hopeful thing said to me was that the brain passages which preside over the intelligence were not affected. Everything else had changed.

But I said to myself, "Nothing has changed! I'm the same person that I was. By prayer, I am still communicating with the same Person. I belong to the same unshakable Kingdom and the same unchanging Person. Nothing has really changed except my means of communicating with the outside world." . . .

I have spent these months looking into the face of Jesus with an unobstructed gaze and what I see is wonderful. It is redemptive, satisfying, and exciting.

"That one dear face, far from vanishing, rather grows; Becomes my universe that feels and knows."[11]

Zechariah's spontaneous song reflected his nine months of reflective silence. Disability can yield creative productions! It was the recovering Zechariah who penned the beautiful Christmas poem known now, centuries later, as "The Benedictus."

God's Acceptance Bolstered Zechariah

Zechariah's poem was a reflection of his theology. He attributed salvation to the work of God. What sustained him through his various vexations in life was God's acceptance of him.

Life has its ups and downs, its crises and catastrophes, its gains and pains, its good and bad times. But life's tough spots become bearable when we have the confidence that all is right between us and God, that God has forgiven us of our sins. Troubles in life are hard to endure, but when our standing with God is on a secure basis, when we are accepted and loved by him, we can endure the slings and arrows of outrageous fortune.

The greatest blessing in life is not children. And by saying this I am not minimizing the joy that children bring into a home. There is no question that they contribute abundantly both to the quality and quantity of life. They are additional companion-friends, bringing happiness to us as we stay in close contact with them.

But there is a dimension that children cannot add. We cannot expect to be accepted by God because we have been good parents. Our eternal destiny does not hinge on marital loyalty and paternal skills. We cannot point to anything we have or have not done to warrant our acceptance by God. The main question is not how good our lives have been, nor how many children we have had, nor what has become of them, but—*are we children of God?*

The supreme frustration—rejection by God—awaits everyone who trusts his or her own goodness to earn a place in heaven. That one frustration will become the worst frustration, for it will be prolonged and irreversible. Hell is a place of eternal frustration. Hell is isolation from all one's friends. Hell is having a lot to say, but not having the opportunity to speak, nor friends to hear.

One of the great blessings of trusting our lives to Christ is that though earthly frustrations surround us, the center of our existence is tranquil because we have been reconciled to God and count upon his righteousness alone as our salvation.

No matter what our age, we can enjoy a God-initiated and God-perpetuated standing. "The knowledge of salvation through the forgiveness of sins, because of the tender mercy of our God" is a joy that the worst disappointments of life cannot destroy.

Things to think about:

1. If you are employed full-time, have you reached a plateau or do you continue to feel challenged? If retired, how did you find the transition from full employment to retirement? How are you making progress in this adjustment? What helps? What hinders?

2. How does the security of knowing you are God's child help you face the disappointments in your life?

13

Simeon: A Senior Blessed by Vision

In order to make a success of old age, one must begin it earlier,
and not try to postpone it as long as possible.
PAUL TOURNIER, *Learn to Grow Old*

We must not rob the years after sixty-five of their value.
You do not need to give up on living at sixty-five
and snooze in a rocking chair.
Too many Americans withdraw into inactivity.
Then they find themselves depressed
and plagued with poor health.
C. EVERETT KOOP, M.D.,
former Surgeon General, *Koop,* **1991**

SIMEON WAS UNDOUBTEDLY ELDERLY. GOD HAD ASSURED him he would not die until he had seen the Messiah. He was a key senior figure in showing the infant Jesus to the world. His story is found in Luke 2.

Misconceptions about Aging

The inclusion of seniors in the Christmas narratives reminds younger readers that God's favor is not confined to the young virgin but includes also the elderly.

Misconceptions about aging fly thicker than migrating geese. The conclusion that anyone over sixty-five is a dullard doesn't hold up. Chronological age does not establish a person's biological age. Society's worst bias is to assume that a wrinkled face means a weak mind. The physically slow are not necessarily mentally infirm.

Murray Seasongood, Mayor of Cincinnati from 1926-1929, was interviewed in his law office at the age of ninety-five. The interviewer asked him, "How do you feel when you wake up in the mornings?" His nonclinical answer: "Surprised!"

"There is little information on how to treat the problem of old age in the Bible, because in the Bible old age is not a problem. Rather, old age is consistently treated as a blessing."[1]

Time is making us face senior issues, because society is aging rapidly. Get ready. The number of those sixty-five years old and over will double in twenty years. And within the "over sixty-five" group, the fastest-growing segment will be those eighty-five and older. Seniors don't need to be over-medicated—or over-isolated. They can still be a useful part of the community.

Scripture helps us face the aging process from its unique perspective. One way to prepare ourselves for old age is to take a second look at some of the seniors in the Christmas narratives and see how they contributed and why. They were an important part of Jesus' infancy. Consider Simeon.

Simeon Was Eager

Luke 2:27 records, "Moved by the Spirit, [Simeon] went into the temple courts." He may not have skipped up the steps, but neither did he excuse himself from going to the temple.

"Moved by the Spirit [Simeon] went." Too many seniors sit around their homes like potted plants. They could be active. They also could both prolong and enrich their lives by making the church, not the bingo parlor nor the senior center, their favorite place.

I'll never forget a retired couple I visited when I was a thirty-year-old pastor. They told me they physically weren't able to attend church, but they would give me their envelopes. I accepted their explanation as having some medical justification. I quickly saw, however, that it was an excuse, for in the following week, guess who was walking past the church pulling her wheeled grocery cart? Mrs. So-and-So, who said she couldn't walk to church.

Mobility will be lacking when motivation is lacking. Some seniors need not only vitamin injections, but also a shot of spiritual dynamism such as Simeon possessed.

Simeon was not feeble. He climbed the steps and showed enough stability that Mary trusted him to hold baby Jesus. He didn't stand off to one side, waiting for the young family to notice him and by chance show him the child. Instead he showed assertiveness by approaching them. He didn't wait to be greeted; he greeted. Simeon came to worship God, but he also came to fellowship with God's people.

When Simeon stayed behind in the temple that day, he was approaching strangers. Joseph and Mary were from out of town, unknown by anyone in the temple unless they had come with some distant relatives. But that was no drawback, for Simeon did not stand apart, afraid to approach "strangers." Imagine: what if he hadn't mingled with the other worshipers? He would have missed meeting that wonderful baby!

Simeon showed by his presence and by his participation that he had not succumbed to self-pity. He had the confidence that he was not going to die without seeing the Messiah. If he shared that hope with others, they may have dismissed his conviction as a baseless dream and unrealistic hope.

Too many retired folk keep to themselves. "They feel themselves to be a dead branch of society, like the remnant at the end of a roll of cloth, sold off cheaply."[2] They wouldn't feel so cut off if they would become more involved in a church family.

Simeon set us an example. He praised God, rejoicing with those who rejoiced.

> Some hearts grow old before their time;
> Others are always young.
> 'Tis not the number of the lines,
> On life's fast filling page.—
> 'Tis not the pulse's added throbs,
> Which constitute their age.
> —*Unknown*

Simeon Was Optimistic

Simeon probably fought the "Bothersome Bs" that come to seniors—baldness, bifocals, bridges, bursitis, bulges, bunions. Another "B" that seniors must fight is bigotry, not just bigotry against their age, but bigotry against others.

Simeon spoke positively and poetically. He made a contribution two ways. First, he uttered the hymn, known as the "Nunc Dimmitis" (from the starting words of the Latin version of the poem), in which Christ was hailed as glorious. Secondly, in his poem-oracle he predicted that Jesus would encounter trouble, yet raise the fallen.

In his canticle Simeon combined both personal satisfaction about holding the Savior and spiritual conviction that Jesus held the destiny of vast numbers, Gentiles and Jews. He made a profound statement, a prophetic anticipation in which we share:

> For my eyes have seen your salvation, which you
> have prepared in the sight of all people, a light
> for revelation to the Gentiles and for glory to your
> people Israel. *Luke 2:30-32*

It is important to notice that Simeon's poem was not a prayer. Simeon was not petitioning God. He wasn't asking to die but was acknowledging that God permitted him to experience that moment. He was sure and satisfied. He spoke of Christ's triumph through truth. There was no doubt in his mind that Jesus would reveal and save.

Another important feature about his statement was how totally he avoided the bigotry of fellow Jews. Jesus' mission included all of humanity, not just the Jews. That was an enormous admission for a devoted Jew like Simeon to make. Israel would be blessed by Jesus' coming, but so also would the world. The Messiah's cosmopolitan focus was strongly stated by Simeon, who could have just as easily succumbed to narrowness and nationalistic pride. How many older folks do we know who seem to have grown more narrow-minded with the years? In contrast, Simeon's view widened. In greeting the infant Savior, he was greeting people of other nations, times, and races, whom he would never see or understand.

This dear old saint was able to see the broader picture. His vision was clearly futuristic and wide-angled. Notice that he mentioned the benefits of Jesus to the world before he mentioned the benefit to Israel!

To most Jews, Gentiles were a real pain—to put it mildly. And anybody connected with the Gentiles was spoken of with disparagement. Take Galilee. Being close to Gentile nations to the north, Galilee was put down. "Galilee, land of the Gentiles" was a pejorative expression. As far back as the eighth century B.C., Galilee had the nasty nickname "land of the shadow of death" (Isaiah 9:2). In the eyes of southern Jews the north was not worth much to Judaism. Those in Galilee were benighted people, "living in darkness." Gentile influence and subjugation there had been continuous from the times of the judges.[3]

Simeon got his outlook on Gentiles from the book of Isaiah, whose prophecies he doubtless poured over. For it was in Isaiah that the worldwide scope of the Messiah got special stress (cf. Isaiah 42:6 and 49:6). "The consolation of Israel" would also bring consolation to people from every tongue, tribe, and nation.

Simeon could have been strongly influenced by the Gentile Romans, who were rough and ruthless in their handling of Jews. In addition to the thundering cruelty of Herod the Great, Simeon probably lived under Pompey, who first captured Jerusalem in 63 B.C. when many were slaughtered. Simeon also would have been alive when the Roman ruler Crassus robbed the temple in 54 B.C. And he was one of the lucky ones Crassus did not deport as a slave in 51 B.C.[4]

Simeon had seen a lot of Gentile viciousness, yet he did not harbor ill-will. The Holy Spirit had a greater influence on Simeon than the spirit of the Jewish world. Luke 2:25 uses the imperfect tense when describing the Spirit's control of Simeon, not as a sudden gripping of the man but a constant and continuous influence. He was a man of the Spirit who would allow neither the tenor of the times nor the tendencies of his race to override the clear directives of Scripture. The Spirit guided his thinking as well as his actions.

Simeon Was Diligent

How had Simeon escaped the provincialism of his contemporaries? Why had he eagerly embraced the conquest of the nations by Christ?

I think the answer is that he knew his Bible. Simeon quoted Isaiah in his hymn. The expression "a light for the Gentiles" occurs twice in Isaiah (42:6 and 49:6). And Isaiah explained that the divine light was meant for "salvation to the ends of the earth."

Simeon was mastered by Isaiah's outlook. He was involved with Scripture on a personal level, and his mental resilience was probably due to his daily reading of the Bible. Simeon's story can inspire us to read and absorb the substance of Scripture.

Simeon's example goes against the current opinion that absorbing Scripture needlessly taxes the hearer. A church member once said to me that the purpose of going to church was *not* to learn, but to meditate, and the minister should not teach but verbalize what the congregation felt.

The previous evening I had read in my copy of Baxter's *Reformed Pastor* a comment that related to that issue. I happened to have the book with me, so I shared the following from Baxter:

Convince [the aged] how impossible it is to go the way
to heaven without knowing it, when there are so many
difficulties and enemies in the way; and when men
cannot do their worldly business without knowledge,
nor learn a trade without an apprenticeship. Convince
them what a contradiction it is to be a Christian, and
yet to refuse to learn; for what is a Christian but a
disciple of Christ? . . . And he that refuseth to be taught
by his ministers, refuseth to be taught by [Christ]: for
Christ will not come down from heaven again to keep
school and teach them under him. To say, therefore,
that they will not be taught by his ministers, is to say
that they will not be taught by Christ; and that is to say
they will not be his disciples, or no Christians.[5]

If you are retired or nearing it, read and relish this and
other Christian classics. Eventually, boredom becomes a
chief problem in retirement. Don't just talk about the
books you plan to read and the places you plan to visit.
Get active in these pursuits *before* you retire, or else you
will not have the energy, skill, confidence, and drive to
do them once you *are* retired. If Simeon read in retirement, it was because he read when he was hard at work.
He read during his vigorous years so that he did not lose
the habit when he grew old.

Leisure invigorates to the extent that we are active.
Idleness kills. Idleness tortures those who are alive
enough to know that they are missing out on the fun. We
must raise our creative and cultural levels. And what is
the dip stick for measuring our involvement? We can
check our progress by asking, "Have we kept in touch
with God's people, and are we challenging our minds
with serious reading?" I believe these two factors help
explain Simeon's bright outlook, his perceptive analysis,
and his satisfying retirement.

The best preparation for retirement is to progress toward it before it arrives. Circulate; don't vegetate. Go to church, mingle with God's people, volunteer for service. Don't drop out of church; drop in.

Simeon took Jesus up in his arms and blessed God. His arms may have trembled as he held the infant Lord, but he shook more with joy than because of age.

We imitate Simeon every time we take up the Bible to read, for Scripture carries Christ. Let's not handle the Bible the way a bachelor handles a baby. The more we pick up the Bible the less awkward we'll be in using Scripture.

Familiarizing ourselves with Scripture and with great books that explain Jesus will make for a leisure that is fulfilling and refreshing. Just as work without leisure is exhausting, so leisure without effort is exasperating. We have many more years of service and great opportunities to witness to and share the knowledge of God.

> Must I be carried to the skies
> On flowery beds of ease,
> While others fought to win the prize,
> And sailed through bloody seas?
> —*Isaac Watts*

Things to think about:

1. Do you sometimes shy away from visitors in your church because you think of yourself as just an uninteresting, elderly

member? What can you do to befriend visitors and make them feel at home?

2. How does Simeon's familiarity with Scripture challenge you? How can Scripture reading enrich retirement?

3. What kinds of cultural narrow-mindedness surround you today that Scripture and the Holy Spirit can help you to overcome?

14

Anna: A Senior Who Faced Grief

At age sixty-five,
the pioneer of modern nursing, Florence Nightingale, wrote:
"Today, Oh Lord, let me dedicate
this crumbling old woman to Thee."

O let my life be given,
My years for thee be spent,
World-fetters all be riven,
And joy with suffering blent!
Thou gav'st thyself for me,
I give myself to thee.
FRANCES R. HAVERGAL

PERHAPS THE ROLE OF SENIORS IS THE MOST NEGLECTED theme in the original Christmas story. Whenever a baby is born the focus is on the child. And the main event of Christmas *was* Christ's birth; it is proper to direct all attention to him who came to secure our salvation.

Nevertheless, a series of seniors entered the picture to reinforce Jesus' specialness. Simeon's canticle, for instance, emphasized the babe's global-saving mission. In addition, he gave Mary and Joseph a glimpse of the ordeal Jesus would endure and of the outrage he would meet.

This child is destined to cause the falling and rising
of many in Israel and to be a sign spoken against, so
that the thoughts of many hearts will be revealed.
Luke 2:34-35

Anna's appearance was connected with Simeon's. She
was probably on hand to hear all that Simeon said. By
divine direction she happened upon the brief meeting of
the holy family. Luke described the encounter simply:
"Coming up to them at that very moment" (2:38).

Anna Was Alone

Anna was old. Her past included a major tragedy—
early widowhood. Luke did not introduce her to
emphasize her age. Rather, her age was incidental to
the length of her anguish and grief. Luke himself must
have marveled at the length of her widowhood and at
her ability to bounce back from losing her mate of only
seven years.

We cannot underestimate the trauma that comes from
unexpected early deaths to spouses. Psychiatrist Paul
Tournier observed:

Widowhood is always a terrible trial, and in addition
to the emotional shock of separation there is always a
considerable disturbance in the social and personal life
of the surviving partner.[1]

When we meet Anna in Luke she is "very old." (The
literal Greek is "advanced many years.") How old was
she? One view is that she was at least 106 years old. This
is assuming that she became a bride at fifteen (not un-
common in that time and culture), was married seven

years, and a widow eighty-four years. Totaled, she was 106 years old on this occasion! Others, however, take the reference to "eighty-four" as the sum total of her age, including widowhood.[2]

I think the over-100-years-of-age option is the preferred view, not on linguistic grounds, but on contextual grounds. Luke's focus was not simply her age, but Anna's heroic attitude in not caving in. She refused to let her widowhood become her defeat. She kept active, and she didn't retreat.

> She never left the temple but worshipped night and day, fasting and praying. (2:37)

That doesn't mean she rented a room in the temple, though; no one except the high priest was allowed to have a chamber there.[3] Matthew Henry speculated that Anna had an apartment near the temple funded by temple charities. The main point was that "she never missed a service."[4] The imperfect tense is used to describe her temple attendance. It meant she kept on "not leaving." She made the temple the original Senior Citizen Center for Jews. Like David, she felt "better one day in Thy courts than a thousand days at home" (Ps. 84:10, NEB).

But Anna was not content with perfect attendance at services—she held her own! She didn't feel that her attendance at the temple fulfilled her responsibilities to God, for she continued with private devotions. Luke's wording: ". . . [she] worshipped night and day, fasting and praying." The normal feast days, sabbaths, and festivals, were not enough; she sought God with the regularity of the rising and setting sun. Anna is a model of worship both public and private as well as a lifestyle of prayer without ceasing, as encouraged centuries later by the apostle Paul.

Matthew Henry commented:

> It is a pleasant sight to see aged Christians abounding in acts of devotion, as those that are not weary of well-doing, that do not think themselves above these exercises, or past them, but that take more and more pleasure in them, and see more and more need of them, till they come to heaven.

Anna was not bitter toward God about her husband's early passing. It was undoubtedly hard for her to return to the temple without her husband, but she persisted. Luke's mention of the length of her widowhood is typical of his sympathetic identification with widows and women. Luke included widows five times in his Gospel.

Self-isolation is a temptation common to widows and widowers. Often they miss the morale their mate once provided. It would seem Anna had the perfect alibi for not going to the temple. She was a widow, she was undoubtedly poor, and she was old. Widowed seniors face the temptation to hide, to withdraw, to stay to themselves. But Anna wasn't going to dwell in self-pity. She wanted to progress in her spiritual life. She was not content to drift along on past memories.

Anna's time alone with God did much to strengthen her and to enable her to cope with loneliness, grief, and loss. Fellowship with the Lord sustained Anna through her difficult years as a widow. In addition to her own contact with God, she had the light of God's presence and the fellowship of God's people to cheer her on. Evening worship was not a chore, but a delight. Her twilight years became spiritual noondays.

When measured years and days must close,
When shades arise as darkness grows,
Come Thou, who knowest all, and guide:
Let sunshine fall at eventide.
The world's high tumult fades and dies,
Sweet silence follows strident cries,
Thou that ordainest all, abide:
Shine from Thy throne at eventide.
—*T. Gwynn Jones*

Anna Was Attracted to Youth

Anna didn't consider age a barrier to meeting and appreciating people. Of course, she would have seen the contrasts between some in her age class and the younger set. Perhaps she would have said a prayer similar to this:

Thou knowest, Lord, I'm growing older;
My fire of youth begins to smolder.
I somehow tend to reminisce,
And speak of "Good old days I miss."
I am more moody, bossy,
And think folks should jump at my command.
Help me, Lord, to conceal my aches
And realize my own mistakes.
Keep me sweet, sane, serene,
Instead of crusty, sour, and mean.[5]

Anna stayed alert. She was spry and quick to notice anything unusual. The expression "coming up to them" (2:38) not only means suddenly but also conveys the idea of awareness. Unlike many her age, Anna was conscious of what was going on around her. She was not lost in memories or so preoccupied with her own feelings that she failed to notice what was happening nearby. And her alertness went beyond physical observation. She caught the significance of what Simeon had said. She was quick to realize that Jesus was extraordinary.

Anna didn't think old. She thought young and would prod any person in her age bracket to discount years and be oriented to the future.

> Time is cruel, but doesn't care,
> It slows the step and grays the hair,
> It wrinkles hands and face and neck—
> How we take it is up to us—
> With much of grace or lots of fuss.
> —*M. E. Bond*

Pensioners are known to guard their independence. They don't want to burden their children or society if they can help it. But they shouldn't allow themselves to scorn interdependence. Different age groups function best with other groups. One way to keep resilient, avoid crotchetiness, and refuse to regress is to keep in touch with youth.

Anna Was Animated in Spiritual Growth

What is the prime tendency in the aging? Physicians note that regression to former days and ways only hastens aging. "As long as you are curious," Dr. Tournier encourages, "you won't grow old."[6] Curiosity about Simeon beaming over baby Jesus caught Anna's eye. And what he said about Jesus struck a responsive chord in her.

During her temple activity, Anna became known for her spiritual insight. Luke described her as a "prophetess." It was not because Anna had the gift of discourse that she was described as a "prophetess," but because she had the gift of discernment. She shared in the prophetic gift not because she could tell the future, but because she was willing and able to bring the Word of God to bear on the present. "To prophesy" in the Old and New Testament sense meant primarily to tell forth, not to foretell. Notice in the story before us, Anna predicted nothing about Jesus, but she did talk about him.

Anna excelled in spiritual understanding. Her perceptiveness allowed her to understand the redemptive tasks Jesus would fulfill in the future. She followed the lead of the Old Testament and concluded that Simeon's identification of Jesus as the Messiah, and his anticipation of his role in the world, were on target.

Her excitement was evident to all, for she left the brief meeting to spread the good news of Christ's arrival.

> She gave thanks to God and spoke about the child to all who were looking forward to the redemption of Jerusalem. 2:38

Anna sensed that Jesus' life would lastingly touch others as he had touched hers. Christ turns an ordinary existence into an abundant life. Anna was animated to share the good news of Christ. So should we.

Our role is much like Anna's. She did not utter any "predictive" announcement about Jesus. Rather, her role was to spread the Word about him.[7] Note, again, that the imperfect tense indicates her continuous enthusiasm. Luke 2:38 says she kept speaking; she habitually spoke of him. She spoke of his work as "redemption." She described a substantial benefit—God's deliverance of humankind from sin.

You are as young as your faith, as old as your doubt;
as young as your self-confidence, as old as your fear;
as young as your hope, as old as your despair.
—*General Douglas MacArthur (1880-1964)*

Anna's audience was primarily with those who shared her hope. She talked mostly with other members of the "Golden Age Club" of the temple and anyone who similarly expected the Messiah's coming. Apparently, there was "a nucleus of old saints in Jerusalem preparing for the coming of the Messiah."[8]

But her words were far more than "old woman's gossip." Gossip is hearsay. Her message was *gospel*, for she had actually met Christ. The infant Christ made her radiant, and she was overjoyed with the prospect of his life. Exuberance marked her conversation. Elation smoothed her countenance. Jesus came into her life, and with his coming came resilient pleasure and joy.

Anna Was Rejuvenated Late in Life

George Eliot wrote a classic novel about a gaunt, weathered bachelor named Silas Marner, a weaver. He lived alone in the village of Raveloe and daily plied his trade.

Silas had two major trials in his life. One was that townsfolk suspected he was a thief. Though no proof was ever presented to substantiate the charge, Silas felt isolated from the citizens of Raveloe. He kept to himself and rarely ventured from his cottage, where his loom dominated the main room. The other trouble came when someone stole his collection of gold coins.

Money was everything to Silas. He could endure the icy stares of the people of Raveloe, but being robbed took away the one thing that gave him pleasure—money.

With his money gone, he had lost all reason to live. Then, on New Year's eve, a golden-haired baby girl was out in a storm with her narcotic mother, Molly Farren. The mother died, and the child miraculously crawled her way to Silas's door.

The golden-haired girl, named "Eppie," changed his life.

The gold had asked that he should sit weaving longer and longer, deafened and blinded more and more to all things except the monotony of his loom and the repetition of his web; but Eppie called him away from his weaving, and made him think all its pauses a holiday, reawakening his senses with her fresh life.

"Eppie" revived Silas in the depth of his dead and dreary soul. She had delivered him from an "insectlike existence."

As her life unfolded, his soul, long stupefied in a cold, narrow prison, was unfolding too, and trembling gradually into full consciousness. . . . Everywhere he must sit a little and talk about the child, and words of interest were always ready for him.

We could hardly compare an old miser like Silas Marner to godly Anna. But the sudden appearance of the Christ child in Anna's life must have been just as rejuvenating as Eppie's presence was to old Silas. Neither one could be silent about their great finds.

When Eppie was grown, Silas said to her:

My precious child, the blessing was mine. If you hadn't been sent to save me, I should ha' gone to the grave in my misery.[9]

When we take Christ into our hearts we find the same to be true; he has saved us from a miserable grave. Seniors who feel the grave to be much closer and more tangible than ever can especially take comfort in Christ's life-giving presence.

Anna Had Invested Her Years Well

One enduring quality of Anna's life was her spiritual dedication and daily contact with God. Because she had fellowshipped closely with the Lord during the long years of her widowhood, her discerning sensitivities sharpened her recognition of Jesus' identity and her appreciation of his redemptive mission. If the religious leaders in Jerusalem thirty-three years later had really been exposed to God's holy presence as Anna was, they would have understood their utter sinfulness and may have seen Jesus for who he was—the only Savior, their Savior.

Anna's story is another instance that knowing God brings benefit in old age—and tremendous surprise with it! We can imagine that Anna's walk after seeing the Christ child was considerably full of zip; weary bones suddenly skipped in joy. Her testimony to Jesus may have made a real "spectacle" among all the solemn folks in the temple. Maybe they thought that "their" aged prophetess had a manic, hysterical attack. (She was ecstatic with God's revelation.) She and the Lord, Simeon, Mary, and Joseph shared a secret that would heal hearts in a wounding and wounded world. God used a somewhat wrinkled saint to bring the soothing message of the gospel. He wants seniors today to be engaged in the same exhilarating enterprise.

Things to think about:

1. Widows and widowers may find returning to church a painful experience. Have you ever talked with someone who found going back to church difficult? What healing steps help a person re-enter church life after a painful loss?

2. How do you think Anna got over her grief?

3. Can you think of a widow or widower with whom you could make contact to ease his or her pain of loss?

4. What advantage does the modern senior have over Anna in terms of contact with Christ? In what ways has Christ brought us hope for the future?

A Senior Prayer

HEAVENLY FATHER,
I truly enjoy life. You have given me innumerable pleasures and many friends, but I am puzzled why others I have loved have left life so quickly, like stones skipped off a stream. You want me to continue to be an instrument for righteousness and I wish to be the most useful servant that you would have me be.

Deliver me from self-pity and complacency. Give me a thankful heart in all circumstances. Enable me to experience your creative energy. Grant me a continued interest in your world and help me to improve my immediate surroundings with a Christlike disposition and with the light of his gospel. In facing trying delays I need your patience and wisdom in how to cope.

Make me persuasive and pleasant, cheerful and courageous in sharing my faith. Equip and empower me to witness to your saving love revealed in the Jesus of the Scriptures.

May my words be kindly phrased, biblically informed, and spiritually compelling. Use my life to be an encouragement and recommendation. Make me exemplary, strong, buoyant, and positive. May my speech be steady and my mind clear so those who listen will not dismiss what I say as unenlightened superstition and empty pious sentimentality.

Deliver me, O Lord, from the blabbering so often ascribed to seniors. Keep me from thinking that people are looking for my comments on those parts of life I know nothing about. Spare me from making a fool of myself, lest I make a mockery of senior life. Make me thoughtful but not moody, spirited but not meddlesome, perceptive but not grouchy, independent but not abrasive, spiritual but not sappy, happy but not superficial, agreeable but not gullible, capable but not haughty.

Lord, I thank you for the lessons I have learned from the lives of the scriptural seniors explored in this book, whose faith and fortitude are an inspiration to me. May my life be flavored by theirs. Give me the insight to rethink my ways in the light of theirs. Enable me to honor Christ and be a blessing to others. Grant me a life open to your Word and serviceable in your church and world.

All this I pray, through Christ, my Savior, Amen.

Notes

Chapter 1: Secrets of Long Life

1. *New York Times*, 12/9/79, A-67; *New York Times*, 6/24/79, A-34; *Newsweek* 2/28/77; *Cincinnati Enquirer*, 9/30/83, A-14; David O. Moberg, "Aging, Christian View," *Evangelical Dictionary of Theology*, edited by Walter A. Elwell (Grand Rapids, Mich.: Baker Book House, 1984), p. 22.

2. *Time*, 7/23/56, p. 55.

3. ABC-News, "PrimeTime Live" (Show #209), September 5, 1991, Susan Adams, Producer; Diane Sawyer, (ABC News, "PrimeTime Live," Journal Graphics, Denver, Colorado). Hungarian pharmacologist, Jazseph Knoll, developed Deprenyl. See the valuable articles in *Consumer Reports*, January, 1992: "Can You Live Longer? (What Works and What Doesn't)" and "Stretching the Lifespan: Less Food, More Years?"

4. Susan H. McFadden, "Authentic Humor as an Expression of Spiritual Maturity in Later Years," *Journal of Religious Gerontology*, Vol. 7, No. 1/2, Binghamton, New York: The Haworth Press, 1990, p. 138. In a 1967 study of several hundred American centenarians, one prominent characteristic was humor (Alex Comfort, *Say Yes to Old Age* [New York: Crown Publishers, Inc., 1990], p. 51).

5. ABC-News, "PrimeTime Live" (Show #209), ibid.

6. W. Somerset Maugham, *The Summing Up* (New York: Signet Classics, 1938, 1964), p. 180.

7. *Newsweek*, 4/23/73.

8. *Time,* 8/3/70, p. 52.

9. George Santayana, *The Middle Span* (New York: Charles Scribner's Sons, 1945), p. 111.

10. James Strachan, *Hebrew Ideals* (Edinburgh: T & T Clark, 1902), Vol. 1:196-197.

11. *Time,* 7/23/56, p. 55.

12. Linda Goodman, *Star-Signs* (New York: St. Martin's Press, 1987), p. 418.

Chapter 2: Biblical Records of Long Life

1. See William Henry Green, "Primeval Chronology," *Bibliotheca Sacra,* Vol, 47 (1890), pp. 285-303, reprinted in *Classical Evangelical Essays in Old Testament Interpretation,* edited by Walter C. Kaiser, Jr. (Grand Rapids, Mich.: Baker Book House, 1972), pp. 13-28.

2. Paul Tournier, M.D., *A Doctor's Casebook in the Light of the Bible* (London: SCM Press, Ltd., 1954), p. 123.

3. Ronald Youngblood, editor, *The Genesis Debate (Persistent Questions about Creation and the Flood),* (Grand Rapids, Mich.: Baker Book House, 1986, 1990), pp. 166-183. See also p. 314, F. Nolan, *The Analogy of Revelation and Science* (Bampton Lectures, 1833) for Egyptian vs. Hebraic calculation/tabulation.

4. John C. Whitcomb, Jr., Henry M. Morris, *The Genesis Flood* (Philadelphia, Penn.: The Presbyterian and Reformed Publishing Co., 1966), pp. 23-29, 39-405 (on effects of radiation and longevity).

5. Joseph C. Dillow, *The Waters Above* (Earth's pre-Flood Vapor Canopy), foreword by Henry M. Morris (Chicago: Moody Press, 1981), 479 pages. (This is a fascinating book and viewed as a plausible scientific model of pre-flood earth.) The author's work is a revision of his theological doctoral dissertation. Dr. Dillow lives and works in Vienna, Austria.

Chapter 3: Job

1. John Calvin, *Sermons from Job* (Grand Rapids, Mich.: Baker Book House, 1952), p. 5.

2. See John L. Gilmore, "Love Is Creating Products to Raise Funds," *Sunday Digest* (David C. Cook Publishing Co.), June, July, August, 1975.

3. Peter J. Kreeft, *Heaven* (San Francisco: Harper and Row Publishers, 1980), p. 115.

4. Edward Robinson, *Hebrew, English Lexicon* (William Gesenius) (London: Wiley & Putnam, 1844), p. 357.

Chapter 4: Abraham

1. ABC-News "PrimeTime Live" (Show #209), Sept. 5, 1991.
2. Robert B. Girdlestone, *Synonyms of the Old Testament* (Grand Rapids, Mich.: Wm. B. Eerdmans Publishing Co., 1897), p. 32. Similarly, Geerhardus Vos, *Biblical Theology* (Grand Rapids, Mich.: Wm. B. Eerdmans Publishing Co. 1954), p. 96.
3. Philip E. Hughes, *The Divine Plan for Jews and Gentiles* (London: Tyndale Press, 1949), p. 9.
4. John Bunyan, *Grace Abounding* (Grand Rapids, Mich.: Zondervan Publishing House, 1666, 1948), pp. 94-95.

Chapter 5: Sarah

1. Harold J. Ockenga, *The Women of the Bible* (Grand Rapids, Mich.: Zondervan Publishing House, 1972), p. 21.
2. James Strachan, *Hebrew Ideals* (Edinburgh: T & T Clark, 1902), Vol. 1:88.
3. George Bush, *Genesis* (Minneapolis, Minn. James & Klock, Publishing Co., 1860, 1976), Vol 1:290.
4. Franz Delitzsch, *Genesis* (Minneapolis, Minn.: Klock & Klock Publishing Co., 1888, 1978), Vol. 2:43; Marcus Dods, *Genesis* (Expositor's Bible), (London: Hodder and Stoughton, 1888), p. 169.
5. Ibid., p. 170.

Chapter 6: Moses

1. Ernest Wilhelm Hengstenberg, *Psalms* (Cherry Hill, N.J.: Mack Publishing Co., n.d.), Vol. 3:121.
2. Jean Paul Sartre, *The Words* (Greenwich, Conn.: Fawcett Publications, Inc., 1966), pp. 62-63.

Chapter 7: Caleb

1. The two other "Good News/Bad News" Old Testament speeches are in Judges 7:13-14 and 2 Kings 6:13-18.
2. Bertrand Russell, *The Autobiography of Bertrand Russell* (Boston: Little, and Brown, and Co., 1967), p. 18. It was Exodus 23:2 that Bertrand Russell's mother wrote in the copy of the Scripture she gave him. He wrote later: "Her emphasis upon this text led me in later life to be not afraid of belonging to small minorities."
3. *Time*, Sept. 6, 1976.

4. *Newsweek,* July 28, 1980, p. 10.

5. Herbert Lockyer, *Last Words of Saints and Sinners* (Grand Rapids, Mich.: Kregel Publications, 1969), p. 53.

6. Agatha Christie, *Autobiography* (New York: Ballantine Books, 1978), p. 288.

7. Joseph Belcher, *George Whitefield* (New York: American Tract Society, 1857), p. 465.

8. Emil Ludwig, *Goethe* (The History of a Man), translated by Ethel C. Mayne (New York: Blue Ribbon Books, Inc., 1928), pp. 616-617. Jaroslav Pelikan properly noted the self-salvationist (Pelagian) sentiment in Goethe's lines:

"This noble spirit now is free,

And saved from evil scheming;

Whoe'er aspires unweariedly

Is not beyond redeeming."

Jaroslav Pelikan, *The Melody of Theology* (A Philosophical Dictionary), (Cambridge, Mass.: Harvard University Press, 1988), p. 101.

Chapter 8: Naomi

1. Robert L. Hubbard, Jr., "Theological Reflection on Naomi's Shrewdness," *Tyndale Bulletin,* No. 40 (1989), p. 291.

2. Ibid., p. 286.

3. F. Keil, F. Delitzsch, *Commentary: Joshua, Judges, Ruth* (Grand Rapids, Mich.: Wm. B. Eerdmans Publishing Co., 1956), p. 472.

4. Alexander Whyte, *Bible Characters* (Grand Rapids, Mich.: Zondervan Publishing House, 1967), one vol. edition, p. 204.

5. George Lawson, *An Exposition of Ruth* (Evansville, Ind.: Sovereign Grace Publishers, 1895, 1960), p. 45.

6. Ibid., p. 50.

7. Paul Tournier, *Escape from Loneliness* (Philadelphia, Penn.: Westminster Press, 1962), p. 140.

Chapter 9: Barzillai

1. Matthew Henry, *Commentary on the Bible,* Vol. 2:672.

2. Dinsdale T. Young, *Neglected People of the Bible* (New York: American Tract Society, 1902), p. 96.

3. David Hawke, *Paine* (New York: Harper & Row, Publishers, 1974), pp. 82-83.

4. *Time,* Aug. 7, 1953, p. 16.

Chapter 10: David

1. John Calvin, *Commentary, Psalms* (Grand Rapids, Mich.: Baker Book House, 1980), Vol. 5:100 on Psalm 72, introduction.

2. On the cross Christ uttered seven final words. Of some interest are post-biblical last words by saints and sinners. For those interested, see Herbert Lockyer's *Last Words of Saints and Sinners* (Grand Rapids, Mich.: Kregel Publications, 1969), 240 pages, indexed.

3. Gaius Seutonius Tranquillus, *The Twelve Caesars*, Chapter 2, par. 99. From the New Testament period, a similar love of applause was noted in Herod Antipas (Acts 12:22-24).

4. Alexander Solzhenitsyn, *The Gulag Archipelago* (1918-1956), (New York: Harper and Row, Publishers, 1973), pp. 69-70.

5. John Bright, *The Authority of the Old Testament* (Grand Rapids, Mich.: Baker Book House, 1967, 1975), p. 223.

6. Keith Miller, *Second Touch* (New York: Pillar Books, 1967, 1976), p. 26.

Chapter 11: Solomon

1. The authorship of Ecclesiastes varies. Some conservatives maintain it was authored by Solomon (cf. Louis Goldberg, *Ecclesiastes* [Chicago: Moody Press, 1983], pp. 18-22). Other conservatives deny Solomon wrote it (Michael A. Eaton, *Ecclesiastes* [Downers Grove, Ill.: Intervarsity Press, 1983), pp. 22-24). Interesting features of the book's authorship are discussed by Jacques Ellul (*Reason for Being* [Grand Rapids, Mich.: Wm. B. Eerdmans Publishing Co., 1990], pp. 16-22).

2. Robert Munger, *What Jesus Says* (Westwood, N.J.: Fleming H. Revell Company, 1955), pp. 183-184.

3. Frederick Buechner, *Whistling in the Dark* (An ABC Theologized) (San Francisco: Harper and Row, Publishers, 1988), p. 91.

4. A point-by-point analysis of the poem is provided for those who delight in detailed studies:

Parts
Eyes: "Before the sun and the light and the moon and the stars grow dark and the clouds return after rain" (12:2). Some see this as a graphic reference to senior depression, when the scenery behind and the view ahead is darkened. Others see a reference to diminishing visibility described by reference to the sources and symbols of light or possibly a reference to impaired vision. The cloud after rain some see as a reference to cataracts (medically, the clouding of the eye lens). Another reference to eyes is in 12:3 (". . . and

those looking through the windows grow dim"). Windows here would be symbolic eyes, and eyelids are like shades (12:3), reminiscent of Shakespeare's lines, "These eyes, like lamps whose wasting oil is spent, wax dim, as draw to their end" (*Henry Fifth,* Act 2. Sc. 5; 11. 8-9).

Arms: our watchmen. "when the keepers of the house tremble" (12:3). "Tremble" means the arms are palsied or move without control or violently. Our two arms seem to be referred to in 12:4 ("when the doors to the street are closed . . ."). The Hebrew means double doors, such as were found at the city gates. Another possibility is to double doors at home entrances, such as we have today (storm/screen door and main door). When we hug someone our two arms close around them like the opening and closing of doors!

Legs: our strongmen. ". . . and the strong men stoop" (12:3). Some see in this a general stooping that accompanies aging. The thighs rather than the back may be alluded to, for when they lose their strength they bend.

Teeth: our grinding tools. ". . . when the grinders cease because they are few . . ." (12:3). This text calls attention to lost teeth. When teeth do not meet, then chewing is impossible.

Ears: our shut doors. "When the doors to the street are closed and the sound of grinding fades; when rise up at the sound of birds, but all their songs grow faint" (12:4). Both being hard-of-hearing and being light sleepers seem to be symbolized here.

Hair: ". . . when the almond tree blossoms" (12:5). The almond tree's white blossoms refers to white hair (12:5). Interestingly, in January when the almond blossomed the color was pink, turning to white at the tip, then bleach-white before falling like snowflakes to the ground.

With all the various dyes, rinses, hearing aids, and medications many signs of aging are not as evident and seem to be avoidable.

Functions

Activities connected with the body are conveyed through the functioning of the anatomy. This included the use of the eyes, the arms, the legs, and the teeth.

For example: Erect posture is often lost in aging: "strong men stoop" (12:3). "Grinding" (12:4) or chewing slows. The mention of the sound of grinding (low) may be a reference either to slow eating or slackened chewing. Insomnia is mentioned in the early waking at the voice of singing birds (12:4).

Fear of climbing and going out at night: "When men are afraid of heights and of dangers in the streets . . ." (12:5). As one grows older, balance and strength increase the chance of falling or of not moving fast enough to avoid being hit by faster creatures or moving objects.

Disorders

Receiving Problems: The references to inability to see and hear clearly, as well as chewing, breathing, and swallowing have already been referred to above.

Locomotion: Movement with difficulty is referred to in 12:5—". . . and the grasshopper drags himself along. . . . " Some seniors develop hip problems. The grasshopper that drags his legs signifies walking in pain. Stiffness in the hip joint has a bearing on arthritic conditions.

Nerve Damage: The central nervous system seems to be mentioned in 12:6—". . . before the silver cord is severed . . ." The silver cord is the spinal cord. Topping the spinal column is the head: ". . . or the golden bowl broken . . ." (12:6). The golden bowl is the head. It may refer to the trauma of a fractured skull.

Heart Failure or Aneurism: ". . . before the pitcher is shattered at the spring . . ." (12:6). Medically, the heart is a pump, but in terms of the results of heart action, the pitcher conveys the idea of distribution of blood. The pitcher is the heart. The pitcher receives and dispenses fluid, so the heart receives and distributes blood. The heart's pumping action could be referred to. The cessation of pouring means the heart has ceased pumping. If not the heart, 12:6 could refer to the rhythmic action of the lungs: ". . . the wheel broken at the well." 12:6 could refer to the eerie gurgle in the throat ("death rattle") when the lung continues to expand and contract but the upper organs cannot crank out secretions from the throat and death ensues from suffocation.

5. Cornelius Gilhuis, *Conversations on Growing Older*, translated by C. W. Barendcrecht, (Grand Rapids, Mich.: Wm. B. Eerdmans Publishing Co., 1977), p. 21.

6. Jacques Ellul, *Reason for Being*, op. cit., pp. 286-287.

Chapter 12: Zechariah

1. Leon Morris, *Tyndale New Testament Commentaries: Luke* (Grand Rapids, Mich.: Wm. B. Eerdmans Publishing Co., 1974), p. 68.

2. Alfred Plummer, *The International Critical Commentary: Luke* (Edinburgh: T & T Clark, 1910), p. 10.

3. Edgar N. Jackson, *Coping with the Crisis in Your Life* (New York: Hawthorn Books, 1974), p. 145. "In his relaxed mood he may find it possible to refine his interests, discover new ones, and employ new resources" (Ibid., p. 146).

4. Tim Stafford, "The Graying of the Church," *Christianity Today*, Nov. 6, 1987, p. 20, quoting David Oliver.

5. Leon Morris, *Reflections on the Gospel of John* (Grand Rapids, Mich.: Baker Book House, 1986), Vol. 1:89. (Similarly, Dinsdale T. Young, *Neglected*

People of the Bible, op. cit., pp. 100-101.) Donald A. Carson, *The Gospel According to John* (Grand Rapids, Mich.: Wm. B. Eerdmans Publishing Co., 1991) argued that Nicodemus was being sarcastic and scornful (pp. 190-191).

6. *Time,* Dec. 3. 1967.

7. *New York Times,* Feb. 8, 1981.

8. *Newsweek,* Feb. 28, 1977, p. 52.

9. William Barclay, the *Daily Bible Study Series: Luke* (Philadelphia, Penn.: Westminster Press, 1953), p. 4.

10. One other oblique reference to stroke in the New Testament may be John 21:18, where physical helplessness is mentioned.

11. E. Stanley Jones, *The Divine Yes* (with the help of his daughter Eunice Jones Mathews) (Nashville, Tenn.: Abingdon Press, 1975), pp. 30-31, 125. Win Arn referred to his stroke at age sixty-four (pp. 40, 64, 72-73, 96, 107, 117-118 in *Live Long and Love It* (Tyndale House, 1991).

Chapter 13: Simeon

1. Tim Stafford, "The Old-age Heresy," *Christianity Today,* Sept. 16, 1991, p. 31.

2. Paul Tournier, *Learn to Grow Old,* translated by Edwin Hudson (New York: Harper and Row, Publishers, 1972 [1971]), p. 52.

3. Franz Delitzsch, *Isaiah,* translated by James Martin (Grand Rapids, Mich.: Wm B. Eerdmans Publishing Co. , 1954 [1877]), 1:244.

4. Handel H. Brown, *When Jesus Came* (Grand Rapids, Mich.: William B. Eerdmans Publishing Co., 1963), p. 113.

4. Richard Baxter, *The Reformed Pastor* (Glasgow: William Collins, 1656, 1835), p. 334.

Chapter 14: Anna

1. Paul Tournier, *Learn to Grow Old* (New York: Harper and Row, Publishers, 1972), p. 16. See also ibid., p. 96: "Widowhood is not just a sorrow, it is a solitary sorrow."

2. The adverb, "even unto" allows for the translation "up to as much as." Alfred Plummer, *International Critical Commentary: Luke* (Edinburgh: T & T Clark, 1910), p. 72 says: "That she should be considerably over a hundred years old is not incredible." See also Frederick Godet, *Commentary on the Gospel of Luke* (Edinburgh: T & T Clark, 1870), 1:143. A. T. Robertson, *Word Pictures in the New Testament* (Nashville: Broadman Press, 1930), 2:30. Translations that adopt the over-100 view include James Moffatt, *Good News Bible,* and the paraphrase, *The Living Bible.*

Those who say she was "a widow until 84 years" include *Goodspeed, Revised Standard Version, New English Bible, New American Bible, Jerusalem Bible, J. B. Phillips* paraphrase, *and New International Version.* See Joseph A. Fitzmeyer, *Anchor Bible Commentary: The Gospel of Luke* (Garden City, N.Y.: Doubleday & Company, Inc., 1981) 1:431. Raymond E. Brown, *The Birth of the Messiah* (Garden City, N.Y.: Doubleday & Co., 1977), p. 442.

3. Alfred Edersheim, *The Life and Times of Jesus the Messiah* (New York: Anson D. F. Randolph and Company, 1886) 1:200: "No one, least of all women, was permitted to reside in the Temple."

4. Leon Morris, *Tyndale New Testament Commentary: Luke* (Grand Rapids, Mich.: Wm. B. Eerdmans Publishing Co., 1974), p. 90.

5. Julian C. Hyer, *Dallas Times Herald*, April 24, 1967.

6. Tournier, *Learn*, op. cit., pp. 70, 126.

7. J. Fitzmeyer, *Luke*, op. cit. 1:423.

8. A. T. Robertson, *Luke*, op. cit., 2:31; Godet, *Luke*, op. cit. 1:144.

9. George Eliot, *Silas Marner* (New York: Pocket Books, 1972), pp. 162, 19, 163, 168, 209 (the order of usage).